THE BOOK OF
INVENTIONS

THIS IS A WELBECK CHILDREN'S BOOK

Published in 2020 by Welbeck Children's Books
An imprint of Welbeck Children's Limited, part of
Welbeck Publishing Group
20 Mortimer Street, London W1T 3JW

ISBN: 978-1-78312-601-9

Printed in Dubai

10 9 8 7 6 5 4 3 2 1

Commissioning Editor: Bryony Davies
Managing Art Editor: Matt Drew
Designer: Claire Clewley
Production: Gary Hayes

Published in association with the

SCIENCE MUSEUM

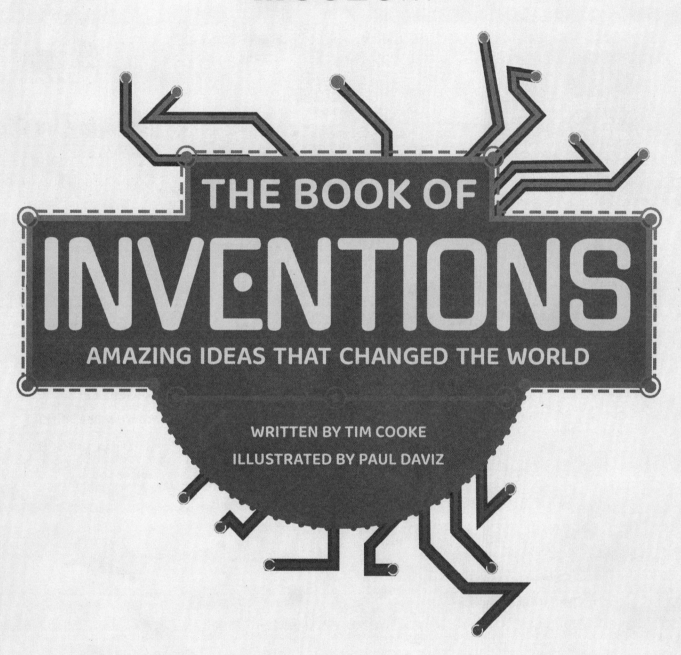

THE BOOK OF INVENTIONS

AMAZING IDEAS THAT CHANGED THE WORLD

WRITTEN BY TIM COOKE

ILLUSTRATED BY PAUL DAVIZ

WELBECK

Contents

1

Giving Us Power
Energy Inventions

2

Taking Us Places
Transportation Inventions

3

Bringing Us Closer
Information & Communication Inventions

4

Making Life Easier
Household Inventions

5

Making Us Better
Medical Inventions

6

Making Us Safer
Accident & Crime-Busting Inventions

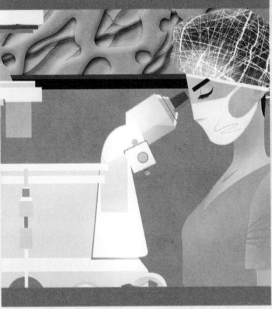

Telescope (c. 1608)

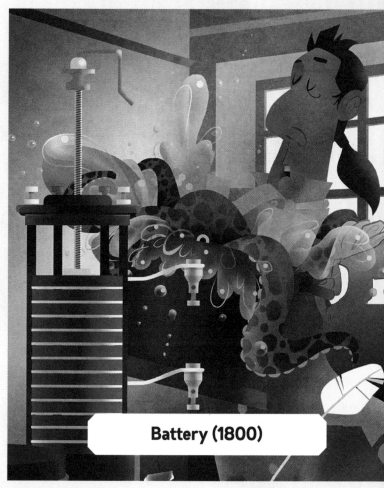

Battery (1800)

Introduction

What is an invention? Put simply, an invention is a creation that didn't exist before. However, just coming up with a new idea isn't enough—the best inventions are really useful things that make a difference to people's lives. So if, for example, you empty the contents of your pantry into a bowl, you haven't invented a new type of food, you've made a mess!

Just because the best inventions are useful doesn't mean each one is a huge leap forward. Not all technological change is the result of a

single invention. It often comes in a series of tiny steps: a thinner spoke on a wheel, a new shape of cooking vessel, a new type of oil in a lamp. Each in itself makes little difference, but over time objects become refined and improved until eventually they are very different from the original.

Sometimes we hear stories of "eureka" moments (*eureka* is ancient Greek for "I've found it"). But often these tales only tell part of the truth. A so-called eureka moment is usually just another step in a series of tiny advances. Johannes Gutenberg is celebrated as the inventor of the printing press, but in fact printing presses were

Dishwasher (1886)

Biofuel from Plastic (2011)

already well established in China. Gutenberg's idea was to use individual pieces of type to make up pages . . . which was in one way just another small technological advance, but in another way an insight that changed the history of the world.

What Is an Inventor?

Today, many people's idea of what an inventor is like is based on history lessons or movies, and it's great—except for the fact that it's often wrong! Inventors are shown as men in laboratories full of test tubes (in history books, virtually all inventors are male), or wild-haired geniuses scribbling equations on blackboards. They're almost certainly not depicted as Egyptian schoolgirls—yet inventor

Azza Abdel Hamid Faiad was just 16 when she invented a way to turn plastic into biofuel in 2011.

That's the great thing about inventions. They have been created by all kinds of people, many of whom are inspired to invent something because they're trying to improve either their own lives or those of others. Take Van Phillips, who did not start inventing until he lost part of his leg in a waterskiing accident in the 1970s. He went on to invent prosthetic running blades to allow himself to keep working out.

It turns out that there's no such thing as a typical inventor—just people who have good ideas and are prepared to put in the work to turn them into reality. Keep that in mind while you read this book.

1.

Giving Us Power

Energy Inventions

People harness energy in many ways, from lighting their houses to powering the International Space Station as it orbits Earth. Sources for this energy vary. Inventors have created ways to use energy from steam, gasoline, natural gas, coal, electricity, nuclear power, and many other sources. There's one problem, however. A lot of energy depends on fossil fuels that will run out sooner rather than later. The race is on to find new alternatives.

Steam Engine

Have you ever watched a teakettle as it boils? If you have, you'll have seen clouds of steam billowing out of the spout. One of the best-known stories in the history of invention tells how a young Scotsman named James Watt watched his mother's kettle boil on the fire sometime in the 1740s. He saw how steam raised the lid of the kettle and realized it was possible to make steam do useful work. That inspired him to invent the steam engine.

It's a great story, isn't it? Sadly, it's not actually true. About 1,600 years earlier, an ancient Roman, Heron of Alexandria, had invented a device that used steam power. Since then, other inventors had come up with their own steam engines. In 1698, the British engineer Thomas Savery used steam to drive a pump to stop mines from flooding. Another Briton, Thomas Newcomen, invented an improved type of steam engine called the atmospheric engine. The first engine of his design was erected in a coal mine in 1712.

By the time Watt came along, the steam engine was not new at all. His version was actually an improvement on Newcomen's.

In and Out, Around and Around

All steam engines are based on the fact that steam expands as it heats up and contracts as it cools. By trapping steam in a confined space and alternately making it hotter and colder, it is possible to make a piston move in and out. Various devices can then change the in-out motion into a rotating motion that could, for example, turn the wheels of a steam locomotive (see page 24).

Watt's big idea was to cool the steam in a separate chamber so that the main chamber did not have to cool down. This made the engine far more efficient. Watt's engine opened the door to a period of almost 150 years when steam power shaped the modern world: the Industrial Revolution.

Changing the World

Unlike humans or animals, the steam engine never gets tired. It was so reliable that it led to a huge growth in industry. Steam engines drove machines that were gathered together in large factories or textile mills. Towns and cities grew up around the factories, where tall chimneys released smoke from the fires that powered the engines. Steam engines were also used to drive locomotives and ocean liners. As a result, people could travel farther and faster than ever before.

3. This large flywheel changes the up-and-down movement of the beam into circular movement. A gear wheel connected to it can power machinery.

1. Steam pushes the piston and piston rod up and down.

2. This huge beam is moved up and down by the piston rod.

Coal-Fired Power Station

Today, almost 40 percent of the world's electricity comes from huge coal-fired power plants. However, the first coal power plant was much smaller—at first it illuminated only 968 streetlights.

Coal-fired power plants burn finely ground coal to boil water. This produces steam, just like the boiling water in a teakettle. The steam spins turbines around. Turbines work like a windmill. If you blow on a windmill, it spins around. That's what the steam does to the turbines. As they spin around, they create an electrical current. So the power plant converts –take a deep breath!–chemical energy (in coal) to heat energy (in steam) to mechanical energy (the turbines) to electrical energy. It's called an energy chain.

A Bright Spark

The first coal power plant opened in London, England, in January 1882. Owned by the U.S. inventor Thomas Edison, it was small enough to fit into a shop, and it powered streetlights on Holborn Viaduct. But it cost too much to run and was turned off after only a few years.

Lighting the World

As electricity was used to light more homes and power more factories, more power plants were built. These were much more successful, and by the early 1900s, large power plants provided electricity for whole cities or regions.
As the years passed, coal-fired power plants were built around the world.

Better than Coal

Burning coal is bad for the environment. We need to come up with cleaner, more sustainable ways to generate electricity. Teenager Maanasa Mendu did just that. She came up with HARVEST, a device that captures the energy in wind, rain, and sunlight and turns it into power. It uses solar cells and piezoelectric materials—materials that generate electrical currents when they vibrate—to do this. Best of all, the device is cheap to make.

Nuclear Reactor

Atoms make up everything in the universe. Your TV, this book, even you—are all made of billions of atoms. Atoms are so tiny they are invisible, and they are held together by large amounts of energy. We can release that energy inside a nuclear reactor to create electricity to power homes and industries.

Before the nuclear reactor was invented, the Polish scientist Marie Curie realized that certain materials released energy. She called this "radioactivity." Her discoveries paved the way for scientists to understand the structure of the atom. And in 1923, scientists learned that it was possible to split atoms in two and release the energy inside as heat.

It's All About U(ranium)

In the 1930s, it became clear that uranium releases the most energy. Some physicists suggested that if you used enough uranium, the atoms would keep splitting in a chain reaction and would create a constant source of heat.

The theory was tested when the Italian Enrico Fermi and his colleagues built a nuclear reactor in a squash court at the University of Chicago. On December 2, 1942, Fermi created a nuclear chain reaction that kept itself going.

Is It Safe?

In 1957 the world's first commercial nuclear power plant was built. Today, there are almost 450 around the world, with more being built. They provide cheap, nonpolluting electricity. However, critics worry that nuclear reactors are unsafe, as accidents could release potentially fatal radiation.

+ Meet the Scientist · Lise Meitner (1878–1968)

Lise Meitner was an Austrian physicist. She and her fellow scientist Otto Hahn worked together in Germany. They were close to discovering nuclear fission (the reaction that releases nuclear energy) when Meitner, who was Jewish, was forced to flee Germany because the Nazi party had risen to power. She communicated with Hahn in secret, and they made their important discovery. But she wasn't recognized for her work—in 1944 Hahn alone received a Nobel Prize for their work.

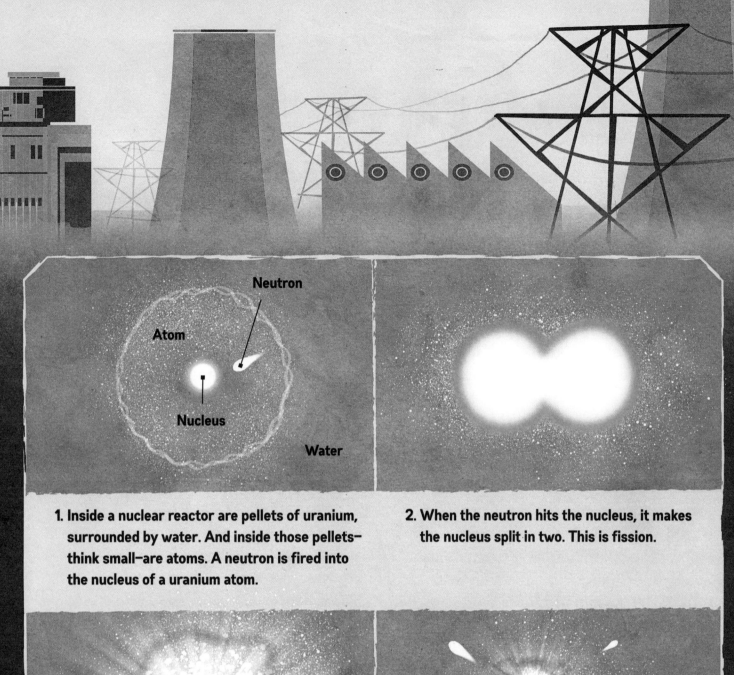

Neutron

Atom

Nucleus

Water

1. Inside a nuclear reactor are pellets of uranium, surrounded by water. And inside those pellets—think small—are atoms. A neutron is fired into the nucleus of a uranium atom.

2. When the neutron hits the nucleus, it makes the nucleus split in two. This is fission.

Released neutrons cause fission in other atoms.

3. Fission releases energy, and it also releases other neutrons from the atom.

4. These released neutrons collide with other atoms and cause fission, beginning a chain reaction. The energy that is released from all this fission is harnessed in a nuclear reactor to give us power.

Biofuel from Plastic

Some of you might not want to read a book about inventions. (Unbelievable, right?) You'd rather invent stuff yourselves. Take Azza Abdel Hamid Faiad from Egypt. In 2011, when she was 16, she invented a brand-new way to make biofuel that could save money and help the environment. And in doing so, she got herself into a book about inventions.

Faiad was still in school when she started to think about two issues facing Egypt. The first was the problem caused by throwing away a million tons of plastic every year. The plastic sits in landfills and doesn't break down. The second was Egypt's use of fossil fuels, which are not renewable. One day, they'll run out.

What's the (Organic) Matter?

One alternative to fossil fuels is biofuels, which are fuels made from biomass—organic matter such as plants or animal waste. Fuels such as ethanol or biodiesel can be produced quickly from biomass. Biomass is also the source for fossil fuels, but they take millions of years to form.

Faiad wasn't the first person to think that plastics could be broken down into biofuels. After all, plastics are made from organic material that was once alive—just like fossil fuels are. But the process of breaking plastics down was slow and expensive. That's where Faiad's brain wave came in.

By experimenting, she found that a mineral called aluminosilicate—a combination of aluminum, silicon, and oxygen—helped break down the long chains of molecules in plastics. It turned them into the gases methane, propane, and ethane, which can be used to make a biofuel called ethanol. The process was quick, it was far cheaper than the existing process, and it also produced more ethanol from the plastic.

In fact, Faiad estimated that her invention would be able to produce $78 million worth of ethanol a year from waste plastic. That's a lot of money in return for a pile of trash!

❓ What Would YOU Do?

Faiad had one idea for recycling plastic. There are other simpler ideas, such as making ecobricks out of plastic bottles. You simply fill plastic bottles with clean, dry waste plastic and then use them for construction. Look around your home for old plastic items. Can you think of good ways to reuse them or change them into something useful?

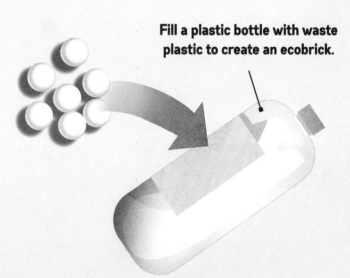

Fill a plastic bottle with waste plastic to create an ecobrick.

Solar Panels

Have you seen solar panels on the roof of a house, or huge collections of them covering the ground in rows—or even on the International Space Station, orbiting Earth? Solar panels are complex devices that convert sunlight into electricity. Earth's supplies of coal, oil, and gas will run out in the next century or so. The Sun will last another five billion years. Which would you rather rely on?

Energy from Light

The idea that light could produce electricity was first tested by the French physicist Edmond Becquerel in 1839. Becquerel mixed chemicals to create a liquid that produced electricity when light hit the surface. This process is now called the "photovoltaic effect" (or "Becquerel effect").

Later in the 1800s, this effect was used to invent the solar cell, which is the basis of solar panels. The American Charles Fritts covered a piece of the element selenium with a thin layer of gold. Light is made up of tiny particles called photons. The gold absorbed photons, and the photons disturbed electrons in the selenium. The electrons moved around, creating an electric current.

Who's Laughing Now?

Fritts claimed that his invention could one day power homes, but people weren't so sure, and the invention didn't take off. At the time there was plenty of coal to go around, so people thought photovoltaic research was a waste of time. However, a few dedicated scientists kept trying to improve the solar cell, such as by using silicon instead of selenium. Then, in the 1970s, the issue became more urgent. The world faced an oil shortage and people realized fossil fuels would not last for ever. Research sped up, and by 2000 the use of solar panels had become much more common.

There is now a worldwide effort to find renewable sources of energy to replace fossil fuels. The carbon dioxide produced when these are burned is a greenhouse gas, which causes climate change. Solar panels produce clean electricity, with no carbon dioxide emissions.

❓ What Would YOU Do?

Some people complain that large arrays of solar panels are ugly. We could only build them in places with few people, such as deserts. But some solar panels have to be built near where people live, especially in small, crowded countries such as the Netherlands. Can you think of a way of disguising solar panels so that they can still receive sunlight but can't be so easily seen?

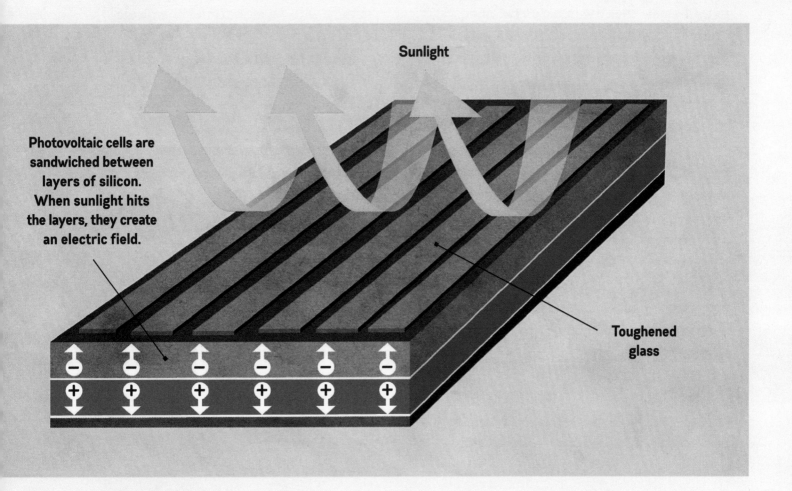

Sunlight

Photovoltaic cells are sandwiched between layers of silicon. When sunlight hits the layers, they create an electric field.

Toughened glass

Batteries

What's the link between a cell phone and a frog's legs? That might sound like the start of a bad joke, but there really is a connection—the battery. In fact, if it weren't for experiments with frogs in the late 1700s, the first battery might not have been invented in 1800 . . . and you might not be able to charge your phone today.

Getting Twitchy

The frogs' legs that began the story belonged to an Italian, Luigi Galvani (well, they weren't actually his own legs, of course). Touching the leg of a dead frog with two different types of metal, he saw that the muscles twitched.

Another Italian, Alessandro Volta, believed that the muscles were twitching because the combination of the different metals produced an electric current. To prove this, he built the first battery.

Volta piled up a stack of disks of two metals, silver and zinc, separated by disks of cloth or cardboard soaked in seawater. When the two ends of the stack were connected by wires, a current flowed. The acidic seawater tried to dissolve some of the zinc. The zinc lost some electrons and became an ion, which then moved through the cardboard disk to regain electrons from the copper. This action generated electricity.

Drying Out

Unfortunately, the chemicals in Volta's stack eventually ran out, and the battery stopped working. That problem was solved in 1859 by the invention of rechargeable batteries. Then, in the 1880s, the German inventor Carl Gassner tried using a paste instead of a liquid to enable the chemical reaction. That led to the creation of the tube-like dry batteries that are still used in many devices today.

❓ What Would YOU Do?

Batteries in cell phones and electric cars need frequent recharging. If you were designing a new battery, what would your priorities be? Should a new battery hold more electricity so it needs less charging? Or should it be more environmentally friendly, with fewer harmful chemicals?

✚ Meet the Inventor · Olga González-Sanabria

Olga González-Sanabria is a NASA scientist from Puerto Rico who has developed the long-life nickel hydrogen batteries that are used on the International Space Station (ISS). The ISS is mostly powered by solar cells, but these only work when the station has access to sunlight. For a third of the time, it has no direct sunlight, and it uses González-Sanabria's high-power batteries instead.

Taking Us Places

Transportation Inventions

What forms of transportation do you take, and where do they take you? Transportation inventions have allowed us to travel farther and faster than ever before. According to one geneticist—someone who studies heredity—the bicycle is the most important invention in history. Why? Because for the first time, it gave ordinary people the ability to travel farther away from their home villages. They met new people—and sometimes married them. That led to more mixing of human genes than ever before. Does that sound a bit far-fetched? Which of the following transportation inventions do you think is most important?

Steam Locomotive

The British engineer Richard Trevithick built the first steam-powered locomotive to run on rails. He realized that existing steam engines (see pages 10–11) weren't powerful enough to drive locomotives, so he began building high-pressure versions.

Along the Rails

Before steam locomotives, railroads were already used to transport goods, mainly in industries such as mining, and to move heavy loads. The rails made the loads easier to pull and kept them on course, but the horse-drawn vehicles were slow.

It took Trevithick several tries before one of his steam locomotives pulled 70 people and a load of iron along a Welsh industrial tramway in 1804. The locomotive only traveled at walking pace, but this marked the beginning of 20 years of rapid developments.

In 1825 a locomotive named *Locomotion*, built by George Stephenson, pulled 450 passengers 9 miles (14.5 km) in about an hour. Stephenson's son Robert later created *Rocket*, the most famous early steam locomotive. *Rocket* could travel 30 miles (50 km) per hour. No one had ever traveled so quickly before.

5. Smoke escapes through the chimney.

4. The steam dome fills up with steam.

3. Tubes inside the boiler heat up and turn the water into steam.

6. High-pressure steam moves the pistons back and forth. Connecting rods turn the wheels.

+ Meet the Inventor · Mary Walton

In New York City in the 1880s, Mary Walton was fed up with noise coming from trains running through the city on elevated tracks. So using a model railroad she built in her basement, she invented a way to use sand to absorb the sound made by vibrating rails. She later sold the rights to her invention to New York City's Metropolitan Railroad.

Changing the World

A great age of railroad building began in Europe and North America in the 1800s. In the United States and Canada, railroads opened up the continent for settlement. New towns and cities were built. People could travel greater distances more safely and cheaply, and goods could be shipped from coast to coast.

2. Burning coal in the firebox creates heat.

1. The tender holds coal and water.

Combustion Engine and Car

The first example of what we would recognize as a car was built by Étienne Lenoir in 1862, using an internal combustion engine. Inside the engine, regular electrical sparks ignited gas inside a chamber to push a piston and make the car go.

Nikolaus Otto greatly improved this kind of engine in Germany in 1876, with a four-stroke engine cycle that is still used today. On the first stroke, a mixture of fuel and air enters the combustion chamber. The second stroke compresses the mixture, which is then ignited by a spark, pushing out the piston on the third stroke, which generates the power. On the final stroke, the piston moves back in to force the used gases out of the chamber as exhaust.

Wilhelm Maybach and Gottlieb Daimler built a car using Otto's engine in 1889. They also invented essential parts of the modern car, including gears and the clutch.

Beaten by the Benz Family
Little did Maybach and Daimler know, but Karl Benz and his business partner and wife, Bertha, had actually beaten them to it!

They had built their own three-wheel internal combustion engine car in 1885.

In a clever attempt to attract customers, and without her husband's knowledge, Bertha took her sons on a 60-mile (100 km) trip across Germany in an improved version of the car. She gained a lot of publicity for the company, and as a result of some of the problems she encountered along the way, various improvements were made to the car. These included adding an extra gear for climbing hills, and introducing brake pads.

Benz's next car, the four-wheeled Velo, appeared in 1894 and became the first car to be produced on a large scale.

All in Line

The U.S. inventor Henry Ford helped make the car the basis of modern life by introducing the assembly line in his factory in 1913. Parts of a car were carried along by moving belts as workers added pieces to them. Just 45 steps and 93 minutes later, there was another completed car.

❓ What Would YOU Do?

Recent car innovations include electric cars that pollute less and do not rely on fossil fuels, and driverless cars that are steered by artificial intelligence. If you were going to invent a new car, what type of innovative technology would you introduce?

Airplane

When you think of flying, you probably think of an airplane, with wings and jet engines. The first time humans flew, however, they were actually in a hot-air balloon, in France in 1783. The airplane followed more than a hundred years later.

The Wrights Get It Right

At the beginning of the twentieth century, two brothers, Orville and Wilbur Wright, built the *Wright Flyer*. It was made from canvas stretched across a wooden frame, with a gasoline engine that used long chains to turn two propellers.

The Wrights used wires to "warp" the wings, or pull them into different shapes. An airplane's wings generate a force called lift. Curving the top side of the wing forces the airflow to change shape, creating lower air pressure above the wing. The air pressure beneath the wing is higher and pushes it up.

On December 17, 1903, the brothers made four short flights on a beach in North Carolina. Orville made the first flight of 12 seconds, but by the end of the day Wilbur had flown for almost a full minute. The age of air travel had begun.

+ Meet the Inventors · Orville (1871–1948) and Wilbur Wright (1867–1912)

Orville and Wilbur Wright used money from their bicycle repair shop in Dayton, Ohio, to build their own aircraft. In 1906 they patented their "flying machine," and in 1909 they formed an airplane company. Wilbur died of illness three years later, but Orville lived until 1948. He advised the U.S. government on the development of aviation. Less well known is their sister, Katharine. She provided her brothers with vital financial and moral support. Wilbur said, "If ever the world thinks of us in connection with aviation, it must remember our sister."

Changing the World

Airplanes changed the world in many ways. Fighters and bombers played an essential role in warfare in the twentieth century. Flight also sped up the delivery of mail, made it possible to ship goods rapidly around the world, and led to a rise in tourism as people traveled farther than their ancestors could have imagined. Explorers such as Amelia Earhart, the first woman to fly solo across the Atlantic Ocean, embraced the invention.

VOUGHT - SIKORSKY
VS - 300

Helicopter

Spare a thought for poor Paul Cornu. This French mechanic designed the world's first aircraft to use spinning blades, or rotors, to lift vertically off the ground. In 1907, Cornu built a machine with twin rotors. When it was ready, he took the controls—but the flight lasted only 20 seconds, and the aircraft fell apart when it landed. Cornu went back to his day job, which was making bicycles.

Saving Pilots

More than 500 years ago, the Italian artist Leonardo da Vinci sketched a machine that would be lifted off the ground by a spinning spiral blade. But it was never built. Cornu's flight, centuries later, showed some of the difficulties inventors faced. To generate enough power to provide lift, rotors must be long and spin very quickly. That also makes the aircraft unstable. Once it leaves the ground, it can easily flip over or spin wildly.

Up, Up . . .

Many different inventors built prototype helicopters in the 1920s and 1930s, but the real breakthrough came in the United States. As a young Russian student, Igor Sikorsky heard about the Wright brothers' invention of the airplane and decided on the spot to become an engineer. He tried designing helicopters, but the technology that existed at the time made them so expensive to build that he had to shelve his ideas.

. . . And Away!

Instead, Sikorsky invented the first four-engined airplane before emigrating to the United States after World War I. He continued to work on a vertical takeoff flying machine. In 1939, Sikorsky designed and flew the VS-300, which had a rotor to generate lift but also a smaller, vertical tail rotor that kept the aircraft stable. (It was tied to the ground in case it went out of control!) He later developed the R-4, which was the first mass-produced helicopter in the world.

Inventions at War

Helicopters have a range of uses, such as sightseeing or rescuing people from remote regions. However, helicopters are particularly popular with military forces. They're used to deliver soldiers or supplies to any terrain or to ships on the ocean. Large helicopters with two rotors can transport tanks and other vehicles. Pilots need to be careful, however—a single Apache Longbow helicopter can cost up to $61 million!

Maglev Train

The fastest passenger train in the world, the Shanghai Maglev in China, reaches speeds of 268 miles (430 km) per hour, without an engine or wheels! "Maglev" is short for "magnetic levitation." The trains use powerful magnets to lift them above the track and catapult them along. The train doesn't touch the track, so there is less friction to slow it down and it can reach very high speeds.

Magnet Magic

Opposites attract—especially when it comes to magnets. A magnet has two poles, north and south. When magnets are placed together, their opposite poles (north–south) attract one another. Like poles (north–north) push each other away. In the early twentieth century, scientists realized that it might be possible to use magnets to make a train "fly" above the ground.

That's Repellent!

However, this idea was only a theory. No technology existed that could create a magnetic field powerful enough to move a train. But in 1967, two physicists in the U.S. cracked the problem. Gordon Danby and James Powell

Electromagnets beneath the train react with electromagnets on a reaction rail to lift the train above the track and move it forward.

patented a way to use superconductors as electromagnets. Superconductors carry much higher electrical currents than normal conductors, so they can generate the powerful magnetic fields used to lift a maglev train above the track and move it forward.

Back to Basics

The first passenger maglev was opened at Birmingham International Airport in England in 1984. But there turned out to be little demand for maglevs. The vast majority of trains still have wheels! Modern bullet trains, which run on ordinary tracks, have become quicker and quicker. For many people, they're fast enough!

All Aboard?

The maglev has many advantages, such as the great speeds it can reach. However, not many countries have wanted to build maglev lines. Most already have normal rail networks and stations. They don't want to build new rail systems from scratch—especially expensive maglev lines. Every mile of the Shanghai Maglev cost more than $60 million.

Drone

Drones—also known as unmanned aerial vehicles (UAVs)—are robot aircraft that fly themselves or are steered by remote control. Today, drones are used for spraying crops, filming extreme sports, and even helping after natural disasters. But a lot of early work on drones was done for a different purpose: warfare.

Aircraft were widely used for the first time in World War I, but piloting warplanes was very dangerous, so radio-controlled aircraft were developed that could fly themselves with no pilots. Signals sent from a handset on the ground controlled the aircraft's movements through an onboard receiver. This was not very accurate, but it didn't need to be, because the first drones were used as targets to practice shooting down enemy aircraft.

Drones became more precise during World War II, when the U.S. Navy attached a TV camera to let the pilot on the ground see where the aircraft were.

Drones Strike Back

There was a burst of new interest in drones in 1982, when Israel used them in a short air war. By the end of that decade, the U.S. military had its own drone: the MQ-1 Predator. With radio signals bounced off satellites, the Predator could be steered anywhere in the world from bases in the United States. Drones could also be programmed to follow a set flight path, filming as they went. A new generation of drones appeared. Some were the size of airliners and could fly for hours. These new drones carried video and still cameras, as well as missiles. Pilots in the United States identified targets on the ground from such high altitudes that no one even saw the drones were there until a missile struck. In the so-called War on Terror from 2001 onward, drones killed many enemy combatants—but also many innocent people.

❓ What Would YOU Do?

Imagine a world in which people have their own personal drones. How could a drone help in your daily life? Could it take your dog for a walk? What kinds of attachments would the drone need, such as a plastic bag for picking up dog mess? Try designing your ideal drone. Does the technology exist to make it possible?

✚ Meet the Inventor · Abraham Karem Born 1937

Abraham Karem is sometimes called the "Dronefather." He was born in Iraq but grew up in Israel. From an early age, he built his own model aircraft. After studying aeronautical engineering in college, he built a drone for the Israeli Air Force. Later, he moved to the United States, where he developed a drone called Amber, which later became the Predator.

Space Rocket

Space is vast. The Moon is a three-day journey away, and spacecraft take about eight months to travel to Mars. And if you're heading to Proxima Centauri, which is our nearest star (apart from the Sun, of course!), the journey will take thousands of years.

In the late 1800s, early science-fiction stories about space travel inspired Konstantin Tsiolkovsky, a Russian schoolteacher who lived in a log cabin. He was obsessed with traveling to the Moon and thought we could get into space using rockets. He suggested using liquid fuel to lift a rocket off the ground, and building a rocket with stages that would fall away during its flight. Tsiolkovsky built many model rockets, but none of them actually worked.

Five, Four, Three, Two, One . . .

The first modern rocket got off the ground in 1926, when the American engineer Robert Goddard launched a 10-foot (3 m) rocket called *Nell*. Powered by gasoline and liquid oxygen, it rose about 40 feet (12 m) into the air before crashing. Goddard's rocket used the same principles as the fireworks used in China hundreds of years earlier. Burning gunpowder in a tube caused gases to escape at one end, pushing the rocket in the other direction.

We Have Liftoff!

During World War II, the German scientist Werner von Braun designed a V-2 flying bomb that used liquid fuel to fly close to the edge of space, 60 miles (100 km) above Earth. After the end of the war, von Braun moved to the United States. He oversaw the development of the rockets that enabled American astronauts to go into space. In 1969 a Saturn rocket designed by von Braun carried the first astronauts who landed on the Moon.

Many people have since contributed to developments in rocket science, such as Annie Easley, an African-American mathematician and programmer who worked for NASA. She worked on NASA's Centaur rocket, which has been used in more than 100 satellite and probe launches.

+ Meet the Inventor · Mary Sherman Morgan (1921–2004)

American astronauts couldn't have gone into space without the help of Mary Sherman Morgan. She was the only female analyst among 900 male scientists, and she didn't have a college degree—but she still designed the rocket fuel that enabled America's launch into space.

3.

Bringing Us Closer

Information & Communication Inventions

Humans are social beings who love to communicate with each other by talking, writing, sharing photos, or instant messaging. Inventions in communication have transformed the way thoughts and ideas are shared: the rise of the printing press in the 1400s produced whole libraries of books; the invention of the television meant huge audiences of people could watch live events. The Internet has revolutionized the way people communicate, from streaming content to social media. But are all these developments positive?

Printing Press

You wouldn't be reading this book if the printing press hadn't been invented. A printing press is a machine that prints words and pictures onto paper, which can then be made into books, newspapers, leaflets and packaging. Before the press was invented, books had to be written out by hand, one copy at a time. This took a very long time and meant they were so expensive that only the very richest people could afford them.

Early Printing

The very first printing was invented more than 1,200 years ago in Asia, where monks would cover carved woodblocks with ink and then press them onto paper. Early movable letter blocks made out of clay were also used in China from the 1000s to the 1200s, but never became widely used. Around the same time in Europe, woodblock printing was also used, but it was still a slow and expensive process.

   All this changed when an inventor named Johannes Gutenberg invented his printing press in Germany in 1450. Although Gutenberg based his press on existing inventions, his improvements allowed books to be printed much more quickly and cheaply. What had he invented? Movable metal type!

Getting a Move On

With movable type, a page of text could be created by placing different metal letters together on a frame. Ink was rolled onto these letters, and a sheet of paper was then placed on top. A heavy slab of metal was screwed down tightly on top, pressing the paper onto the metal letters so that the ink was printed onto the paper. After the page had been printed (or a thousand copies of that page), the individual metal letters could be taken apart and then reused to form another page of text. The old wooden printing blocks only printed around 50 pages a day, but with Gutenberg's new movable type, thousands of pages could be printed in the same amount of time.

Changing the World

Because of Gutenberg's invention, books could now be produced quickly and cheaply enough that middle-class people could afford them. For the first time in history, lots of people could learn to read, and knowledge and ideas could spread more quickly and widely than by word of mouth. Although many poorer people still couldn't afford books or be taught to read, that would begin to change. Over time, more and more people would become part of this information-sharing world.

41

Telegraph

For most of history, long-distance messages could only travel as fast as a person could run or a horse could gallop. Lighting beacon fires or waving flags could also send simple messages (like, "Help, my flag's on fire!"). That all changed in the 1830s with the invention of the electric telegraph. It could send messages across whole countries in seconds—and it changed the world.

The telegraph sends messages along wires by using an electric current. Electromagnets turn pulses of electricity in the wire into magnetic fields. At the destination, the magnetic fields are turned into signals that spell out a message.

Morse Code

Early telegraphs were slow, so the American inventor Samuel Morse tried to invent a better system. He worked with the engineer Alfred Vail to develop a pattern of short and long pulses—dots and dashes—to stand for each letter of the alphabet. Morse persuaded the U.S. Congress to build a telegraph, and sent the first message. The system became known as Morse code—although Vail deserves a lot of the credit for it!

Pointing the Way

The first experiments with telegraphs took place in Spain and Germany. Electrical pulses sent along a wire made magnetic needles swing to point to letters on a chart. That technique was used by two British inventors to create the first practical telegraph. Their device spelled out messages using five magnetic needles on a chart of letters arranged in a diamond shape. (They only included 20 letters—there was no space for C, J, Q, U, X, or Z!) It was in use on Britain's early railroads by 1839.

Coast to Coast

The railroads and the telegraph developed together. The telegraph could do much more than warn if a train was running late. The United States is so vast that it took a week to travel by train across the country. Improvements to the telegraph made it possible to receive the news much more quickly. Together, railroads and telegraph wires helped connect the east coast to the west coast.

❓ What Would YOU Do?

Morse code is just one way to transmit messages by using signals to stand for letters. Can you devise your own code? Think about using emojis on your phone, or a series of colors. Using a different one for every letter in the alphabet would be slow and difficult to remember. Try different combinations of symbols or colors.

Radio

The Scottish physicist James Clerk Maxwell predicted in 1864 that waves of electricity and magnetism—what we now call radio waves—could travel through space. Two decades later, the German physicist Heinrich Hertz proved Maxwell was right. But when Hertz was asked the possible uses of this discovery, he replied, "Nothing, I guess." Which goes to show that even the most brilliant scientists can be dense sometimes!

No More Wires

The telegraph was great, but it required a lot of poles and wires. A wireless communication system would be even better. The Serbian-born American Nikola Tesla developed his own radio system, but the credit went instead to the Italian Guglielmo Marconi. From 1894, Marconi started sending telegraph signals without wires. Soon, he could send radio signals up to 1.5 miles (2.4 km) using a transmitter, a receiver, and two large antennae.

The Italian government rejected his invention, so Marconi took it to England, where it made the British Army and Navy very excited. In 1899, Marconi sent signals from England to France, and in 1901 across the Atlantic Ocean. For the British, radio helped unite their huge empire around the world.

Continuous Waves

Marconi's invention could only carry electrical signals. To send the human voice required a way of producing continuous radio waves. This was invented in 1900 by the Canadian-American engineer Reginald Fessenden, whose voice was the first ever sent by radio. What did he choose to say? "Hello, one, two, three, four."

Radio improved quickly. The American Lee de Forest invented a special valve that amplified weak signals, and Greenleaf Pickard created a radio set that used a silicon crystal to tune in to a particular signal. The first commercial radio show was broadcast in Pittsburgh, Pennsylvania, in November 1920. Within four years, there were 600 radio stations across the country.

Changing the World

Radio made it easier for generals to command their armies and for ships and aircraft to report on their positions. It was also a popular form of entertainment that carried music, drama, and even sports commentaries into people's homes. The earliest listeners used headphones, but after speakers were added in the early 1920s, families gathered around the radio to listen to a world far beyond their walls.

Telephone

On February 14, 1876, a lawyer visited the Patent Office in Washington, D.C., and asked to patent a telephone. (Patents prevent people from stealing an idea.) He represented the Scottish-born inventor Alexander Graham Bell. A few hours later, another lawyer visited the office to apply for a patent for the telephone, on behalf of the American inventor Elisha Gray.

Who Was First?

It seemed as though both men had invented more or less the same thing. Despite Gray's claim, Bell received his patent three weeks later—before he had actually built a telephone. But it was only a few days later that he made the first telephone call to his assistant in the next room. Bell said, "Mr. Watson, come here—I want to see you."

How It Began

Bell was a teacher of the deaf, which made him interested in how hearing works. He believed that if an electric telegraph could carry pulses, then it was also possible for electricity to carry sounds such as voices. Bell soon realized that he didn't know enough about electricity, so he hired the electrical technician Thomas Watson. In 1876, the two men came up with a device in which sound waves from someone's voice caused vibrations in a stretched drum, which moved a spring and magnet that produced electrical charges that matched the vibrations. The charges traveled to the other end of the line, where the process took place in reverse.

I'll See You in Court!

Bell and Watson called their device the telephone. In ancient Greek, *tele* meant "distant" and *phone* meant "voice." Elisha Gray and many other inventors continued to claim that they had invented the telephone. Bell's company fought more than 587 lawsuits over 20 years to protect his patent. Despite the controversy, the device rapidly became popular. By 1900, there were 600,000 telephones in the United States. By 1915, the telephone system stretched all the way across North America.

+ Meet the Inventor · Alexander Graham Bell (1847–1922)

Alexander Graham Bell invented many other devices as well as the telephone. His harmonic telegraph carried multiple messages at the same time. He also designed a speedboat that rose out of the water on wings called hydrofoils, a metal detector, and a machine to help people with weak lungs breathe more easily. He produced an improved version of the phonograph, as well as the first wireless telephone.

Photograph

Would you recognize your favorite movie star, singer, or sports hero from an image alone? Thanks to photographs, of course you would! But imagine only seeing a painting or drawing of someone. If the artist wasn't any good, it might not look at all like the real person. The photograph has changed all that.

The first permanent photograph was taken in about 1826 by the Frenchman Joseph Nicéphore Niépce. Almost a hundred years earlier, the German chemist Johann Schulze had discovered that a mixture of silver and other chemicals turned dark when exposed to sunlight. But Niépce used an oily substance called bitumen instead, and his photograph was a grainy picture of the view from a window in his home. To create this, Niépce used a camera obscura, an existing invention which was a simple wooden box with a small hole in it. Into the box he placed a metal plate coated in bitumen. After a few hours, the areas on the plate exposed to sunlight hardened to create the first photograph.

Say Cheese (Lots of Times!)

Around the same time, Niépce's colleague Louis Daguerre invented a different way to produce permanent images called daguerreotypes. These used a coating of silver to produce images, including some of the first photographic portraits. The subjects had to stay completely still for ten minutes while the chemical plate gathered light. The first commercial camera, the Giroux Daguerreotype, went on sale in 1839. Meanwhile, the Englishman William Henry Fox Talbot invented a way of making many prints from a single image.

Snappier Shots

Photography was constantly improving, but it was still slow and messy. The chemicals involved had to be dried and fixed in place. When the gelatin plate was invented in the 1870s, it was "dry" and more sensitive to light, making taking photographs easier and quicker. In 1889, the U.S. inventor George Eastman invented transparent film, which was made into rolls for use in the Kodak camera. This handheld camera allowed people to snap anything that caught their eye—just like photography today.

Digital Photography

Today, people take more than 1.2 trillion photos every year. Most of them are taken using digital technology. Images are no longer recorded on plates or film, but as a computer file. The first commercial digital camera went on sale in 1981. The same kind of technology is used in the cameras on cell phones.

Television

Turn on the TV and you can catch up with the news, watch movies, or follow sports, all from your couch. It's so easy! Television is highly complex, however, and so was its invention. Inventors around the world worked on different aspects of the device during the 1920s and 1930s.

People spend a lot of time watching TV. In the United States, households watch more than seven hours of TV every day on average. As they watch, their eyes trick their brains. What looks like smooth action is actually a series of still pictures that change more than 50 times per second. Each picture is made up of tiny dots called pixels.

Different Channels

In 1924 the Scottish inventor John Logie Baird used a rotating wheel with holes in it to scan an image as a series of stills. These were transmitted as radio signals and then turned back into images by a receiver. Baird's system was adopted by the British Broadcasting Corporation (BBC), which began regular black and white public TV broadcasts in 1936. By 1937, the U.S. inventor Philo Farnsworth had developed an

electronic system that produced much higher quality images. Meanwhile, the Russian-American inventor Vladimir Zworykin came up with yet another way of producing television signals. In 1954, the first color TVs went on sale.

Tubeless TV

The first screens were based on the cathode-ray tube. In this device, a heated electrical terminal fires particles called electrons at a screen coated with phosphor. The phosphor glows, producing a picture on the screen. Modern high-definition flat-screen TVs work differently. Most are LCD, which stands for liquid crystal display. The liquid crystals allow different amounts of light to pass through them, creating the different colors in the picture.

Changing the World

The television is one of the most far-reaching inventions in history. It allowed people everywhere to witness events such as the coronation of Queen Elizabeth II in 1953 and the Moon landing in 1969. It has influenced politics and business, as politicians have spread their ideas and advertisers have sold their products. It has also educated and entertained generations of people.

Computer

The computer has made it possible to perform complex mathematics easily, but also to process and store huge amounts of information. Who you think invented the computer, however, depends a lot on what you think a computer is.

"Computation" simply means doing math, so any machine that does calculations can be called a "computer." In the 1830s, the British engineer Charles Babbage designed a mechanical calculator called a "difference engine." This intrigued the English mathematician Ada Lovelace, who designed a way to program the difference engine–creating the first computer program.

Computers for Victory

For most people, however, a computer is an electronic device that can carry out tasks and store information in its memory. The first computers of that type appeared during World War II. In 1941 the German engineer Konrad Zuse built electrical computers to make calculations for aircraft designers. Zuse's Z3 was the first fully programmable computer.

In Britain, the mathematician Alan Turing designed a computer to help code breakers crack secret German messages during World War II.

+ Meet the Inventor · Grace Hopper (1906–1992)

Grace Hopper worked on one of these first programmable computers in the United States. But she later went on to invent the first universal computer language, called COBOL. This meant anyone could be a programmer, not just advanced mathematicians! She is also said to have coined the term "debugging"–which means removing errors from computer hardware or software–when a moth got in the computer.

How Very PC!

These early computers filled whole rooms, but they became much smaller in 1947, after the invention of an electrical component called the transistor. It allowed a tiny integrated circuit to contain a huge amount of computing power. Computers got even smaller with the appearance of the first personal computers (PCs) in the 1970s. The computing revolution really took off in the 1980s and 1990s. By 2018, almost 90 percent of households in the United States owned at least one computer.

Internet and Wi-Fi

In a strange time before the Internet, only about 30 years ago, you couldn't stream music or watch cat videos on demand. There are many people to thank for the Internet as we know it today.

The Best Form of Defense

In 1969 the U.S. Department of Defense came up with a system named ARPANET that shared data between computers using phone lines. At first it linked four computers, but it grew quickly. One of the people in charge was the U.S. information scientist Elizabeth Feinler. In 1971

the first e-mail was sent. Three years later, the term "Internet" was first used, and the network became international when servers in Britain, Norway, and Sweden joined. In the 1980s American mathematician Radia Perlman, often called the "Mother of the Internet," came up with Spanning Tree Protocol (STP), which essentially gave traffic rules to the Internet.

The World Wide Web

It was only in 1992, however, that the World Wide Web made the Internet simpler for ordinary people to use. It was created by

Changing the World

The Internet has changed how people learn, shop, and relax. It is vital to advertising and politics. It has also educated and entertained generations of people (although many people are concerned that it also spreads "fake news"). In the future, what is called the Internet of Things (IoT) might change our lives even more. If your refrigerator detects that you are low on milk, it will automatically contact an online grocery store to order more.

British physicist Tim Berners-Lee. In 1990 he built the first website and named his invention the World Wide Web.

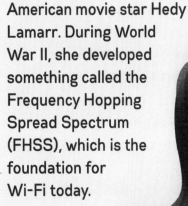

Other people have also contributed to the systems we use. Elizabeth Feinler developed those now-familiar domain names on the ends of websites, such as ".com," ".net," and ".org," plus an early model for e-mails.

+ Meet the Inventor · Hedy Lamarr (1914–2000)

Most people connect their phones or tablets to the Internet using Wi-Fi, without having to use a cable. That is thanks to American movie star Hedy Lamarr. During World War II, she developed something called the Frequency Hopping Spread Spectrum (FHSS), which is the foundation for Wi-Fi today.

Satellites and GPS

While you're reading this, do you know where you are? Not which room you're in, but where you are on the surface of the planet. If you don't know, you can easily find out—thanks to an arrangement of 27 satellites that perform this function, orbiting Earth twice a day about 12,550 miles (20,200 km) above your head.

The satellites are part of the Global Positioning System (GPS). It was put into operation by the U.S. Department of Defense in 1993, but satellites had already been around a long time by then. The first satellite was launched by the Soviet Union in 1957. Named *Sputnik*, the ball-shaped sphere orbited Earth every 96 minutes, using four antennae to transmit radio signals back to the ground.

Space Race

Americans were so startled by the Soviet achievement that they started the National Aeronautics and Space Administration (NASA) to make sure their own space exploration matched that of their Cold War enemies. That started the Space Race that eventually led to humans landing on the Moon in 1969—and to a lot more satellites orbiting Earth. They were used to take photographs of the planet; to study weather; to beam TV, radio, and telephone signals around the globe; and, since 1993, to help navigation through GPS.

GPS satellites orbit Earth in such a pattern that at least four can be seen from any point on the planet. They give out constant low-frequency radio signals. A GPS device detects the four signals and times how long each signal has taken to travel from its individual satellite. This allows it to calculate its exact position on the planet.

+ Meet the Scientist · Gladys West Born 1930

Before GPS was launched, U.S. mathematician Gladys West worked for the U.S. Naval Weapons Laboratory. She was the second African-American woman ever to be employed there. She collected the data from satellites before processing it, to figure out their exact locations, and played an important role in the development of the system.

Crowded Space

There are about 5,000 satellites orbiting Earth. Some scan Earth's atmosphere or surface, studying the weather or changes in vegetation. Others carry telescopes that look deep into space (the telescopes get a better view than on Earth because they're above the clouds and dust of the atmosphere). Many reflect TV and radio signals broadcast from the ground over a wide area. Space has become crowded . . . but so far there has only been one major crash, between a U.S. and a Russian satellite in 2009.

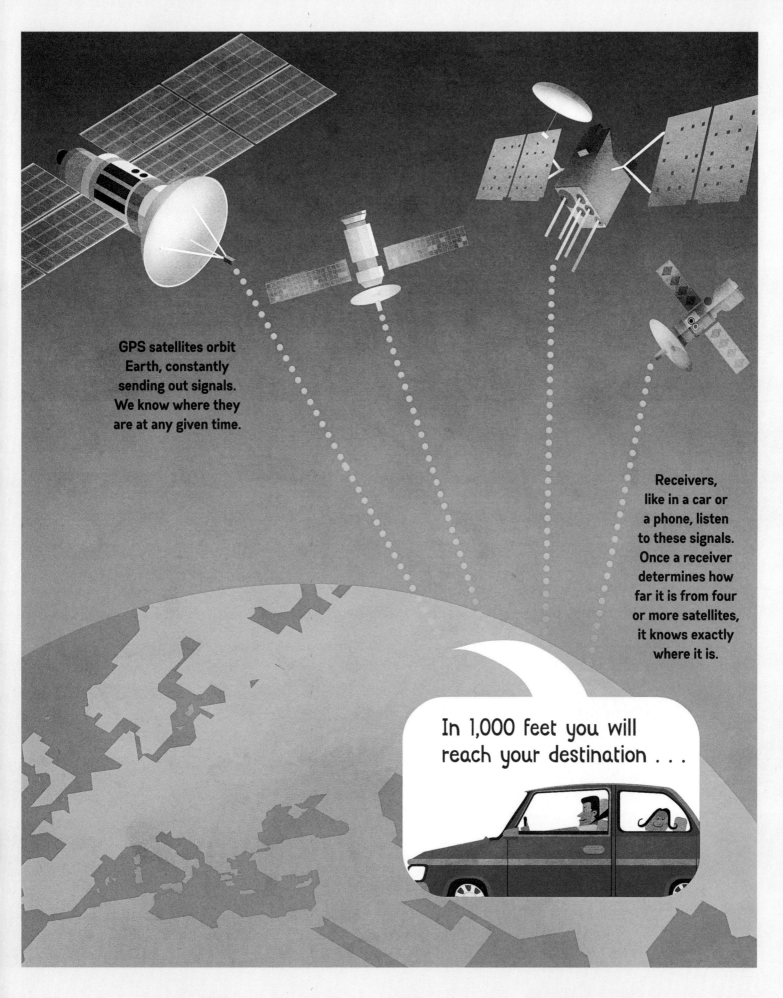

Telescope

Have you ever used a telescope to look up at the night sky? Perhaps you saw craters on the surface of the Moon or the red glow of the planet Mars. According to one famous story, the telescope that made all this possible was inspired by children in the Netherlands shortly before 1608.

The children were playing with lenses made by an eyeglass maker named Hans Lippershey. They discovered that looking through two different shaped lenses made objects seem bigger. Lippershey put the two lenses at either end of a tube and tried to patent his new invention. At about the same time, several other people produced a similar device.

Galileo Builds a Telescope . . .

Whoever was first, word soon spread, and by 1609 people around Europe were building telescopes. The most famous was the Italian scientist Galileo Galilei, who made an instrument that magnified objects by about 20 times. The rulers of Venice paid him a large reward for his invention. They thought it could give them an early warning if enemy ships appeared on the horizon.

+ Meet the Inventor · Galileo Galilei (1564-1642)

Galileo was a great physicist, and the first person to study space using a telescope. He published a theory that Earth might orbit the Sun—but the Catholic Church taught that Earth was the center of the universe. Galileo was put on trial and placed under house arrest.

. . . and Discovers a New Universe

However, Galileo decided to point his own telescope at the sky. He studied the Moon, where he saw mountains and craters. He discovered four moons circling Jupiter and saw black spots on the face of the Sun (though you should never look directly at the Sun). These were exciting discoveries—but they also spelled trouble. The powerful Catholic Church taught that the heavens were perfect. There was no room in their beliefs for what Galileo observed!

Back in Time

Some modern telescopes use receivers to pick up electromagnetic radiation produced by chemical activity in distant stars, and they turn this into images. Radiation from the farthest stars was emitted more than 13 billion years ago, so these telescopes are not only looking across long distances— they are also looking back to a time soon after the universe began.

Making Life Easier

Household Inventions

Look around your home. It's full of inventions that have been designed to make daily life easier. Many labor-saving devices were invented by women, perhaps because for many centuries, women generally took care of the home. While every home is different, and no one yet has invented a robot that will do all the chores, few homes now lack an indoor toilet, a vacuum cleaner, or electric lights. If yours does, check whether you're accidentally living in a cave!

Flushing Toilet

Is there someone in your family who loves to spend a long time on the toilet? Perhaps it's you. In that case, you owe your thanks to John Harington. Or maybe to Alexander Cummings. Or perhaps to Thomas Crapper. Or even to Thomas Twyford. For something that looks so simple, the flushing toilet had a lot of inventors.

One of the first people to have a flushing toilet was the English queen Elizabeth I. The device was a present from her godson, the poet John Harington, in 1596. Harington had a knack for making the queen angry, usually by writing saucy poems. So Harington's present was like a peace offering. His invention had a water tank, or cistern, from which water flushed waste out of the toilet bowl and into a pit.

"S" Doesn't Stand for Smell

The problem with Harington's toilet was that smells from the pit often rose back into the house. The queen probably wasn't very impressed! The smelly problem wasn't solved until 1775, when Alexander Cummings added an S-shaped pipe to the bottom of the toilet bowl. Water in the pipe created an air pocket that acted as a trap for the smells. That was a great improvement—but the S-bend often dried out or got blocked. The English sanitary engineer Thomas Crapper turned the S-bend into a U-bend in 1880, solving the problem.

Around the same time, the British pottery manufacturer Thomas Twyford came up with a new toilet. Instead of the toilet being contained in a wooden box, Twyford made one-piece toilets out of porcelain. This made them easier to keep clean. Between them, Crapper and Twyford shaped the flushing toilet that we know today.

+ Meet the Inventor · Thomas Crapper (1836–1910)

The London plumber Thomas Crapper is often called the father of the flushing toilet, but the fact is that he only improved an already-existing design. He invented the U-bend and added a ball cock to control the flow of water into the tank. Crapper also opened the world's first plumbing showroom. He was so good at promoting his sanitary wares—toilets, bathtubs, and sinks—that his name is permanently linked to, um, bathroom business.

When the handle is pulled, water is released into the bowl, flushing the contents of the toilet through the U-bend and into the drain.

The U-bend stays filled with water, stopping bad smells from coming up the drainpipe.

Home Security System

Imagine this: you're sitting on the couch when the doorbell rings, so you tap an app on your phone to see who it is. If it's a pal, you press a button to let them in. If it's someone with a box, you ask them to leave it on the doorstep. Then you get back to relaxing.

You may not have this app, but it does exist. The inventor you have to thank for it—and for making your home safer—is Marie Van Brittan Brown. She came up with the idea of the modern home security system 50 years ago. She didn't call herself an inventor. She was a nurse. But it was because she was a nurse that she became an inventor (if you see what I mean).

Smile, You're on Camera

In the mid-1960s, Brown was living in an area of New York City called Queens. There was a lot of crime in Queens, and the police struggled to keep it under control. Brown didn't feel safe late at night. People would ring her doorbell and try to get her to open the door. Worse, her husband, Albert—an electronics technician—was often away.

So Brown invented a way to see who was outside from anywhere in the apartment. Her device comprised a closed-circuit camera that moved to look through three or four peepholes in the door. The picture was displayed on TV screens throughout the apartment. There was a button that let Brown talk to whomever was outside, and another that let her lock or unlock the door. There was also a panic button that was wired up to a security guards' office or the police station.

Showing the Way

The device was awarded a patent in 1969. Brown's system formed the basis of virtually all home security systems today.

Surveillance

Since the 1960s, there has been a huge rise in the use of cameras to record people's movements. Some people claim that cameras are necessary to prevent crime, as in Brown's device. Other people argue that people have the right to go about their business in private. They say security cameras are an invasion of our privacy.

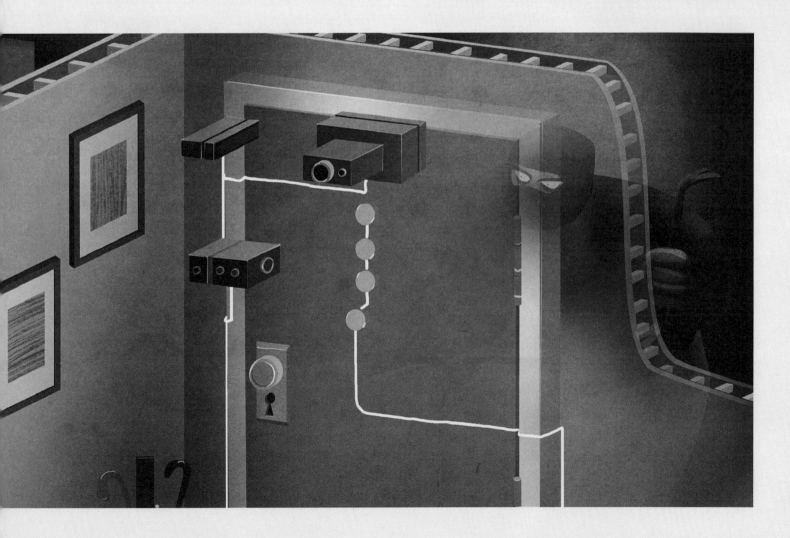

Refrigerator

Imagine life without a refrigerator. It would be difficult to prevent food from rotting. Some foods might not even exist. After all, who wants to live in a world of room-temperature yogurt?

Brrrrr!

Our ancestors learned that keeping food at a low temperature keeps it fresh. (We now know that it's because cold kills the bacteria that make food go bad.) In colder parts of the world, people often stored food with blocks of ice. By the 1800s, ice was shipped around the world to keep food cool in cabinets called cool boxes.

Changing the World

The refrigerator is a great convenience in our lives, but in many ways it is also at the heart of the modern world. Until refrigeration, it was difficult to provide enough fresh food to populations in huge cities. Once refrigerated train cars and ships were developed—which were like large, moving refrigerators—meat, dairy produce, vegetables, and fruit could be transported around the world. This allowed more and more people to live in cities. It also increased the overall health of the population and helped lead to a rise in how long people lived.

Getting Warmer

It was in the early twentieth century that the first home refrigerators were developed. In 1913 U.S. engineer Fred W. Wolf Jr. created a fridge that used the alternate expansion and condensation of sulfur dioxide to remove heat from a cool box. Most modern refrigerators use a similar process. Gases such as ammonia absorb heat from inside the fridge and then release it outside as they expand into a liquid.

Wolf's refrigerator wasn't the only one. In 1914 U.S. inventor Florence Parpart was given a patent for her refrigerator. Parpart was very good at marketing and selling her products by developing her own advertising campaigns.

Another female inventor, Lillian Gilbreth, later came up with a very handy invention—shelves inside fridge doors! She was also responsible for other things you might use at home, such as the foot-pedal trash can and the electric food mixer.

Deep Freeze!

Wolf's refrigerator did not catch on, but one of his ideas did: an ice tray for freezing water. Freezing keeps food fresh even longer than chilling. It became popular after the U.S. biologist Clarence Birdseye watched the Inuits in northern Canada freeze fish deep beneath the ice to preserve them. Birdseye began developing his own way to freeze fish. His first company went bust in 1924, but later that year he came up with a new way of freezing food quickly using a machine that froze small portions between metal plates at very low temperatures.

Plastic and Artificial Fibers

Plastic is everywhere. In 2019, a submarine dived a record 7 miles (11 km) deep in the Pacific Ocean and found a plastic bag on the seabed. Plastic is a harmful pollutant. It takes hundreds of years to break down. But try to imagine a world without it—no plastic bottles or toys, no fleece hoodies. No trainers or bicycle helmets. No spandex gym clothes or fiberglass skateboards. Plastics are everywhere in the modern world—but do they do more harm than good?

Plastics are artificial substances made from organic materials such as coal or petroleum. The first successful plastic was made in 1856, when the English inventor Alexander Parkes was trying to waterproof fabric. Parkes found that plant cellulose and caster oil dried into a hard substance like ivory, which was in short supply. Parkes's new material was a cheaper alternative, although it only became popular after an inventor in the United States, John Wesley Hyatt, came up with an improved version, which he called celluloid. It was first used to make billiard balls.

Plastic Takes Over

Celluloid was followed by a hard plastic called Bakelite, often used in radios. This was the first plastic to be fully synthetic (human made). In the late 1930s polystyrene became popular. Often made as a foam, it comes in hard or soft versions that are widely used for packaging. Plastic bottles became popular in the 1970s, because they were a lighter alternative to glass and did not break. By the 2000s, however, people were worried by the harm that discarded plastic bottles and shopping bags caused.

Wearable Plastic

One popular use for plastics is to make artificial fibers. Viscose was invented in 1891, and in 1935 the U.S. chemist Wallace Carothers created nylon. Carothers was trying to make artificial silk, because the United States' relationship with Japan, its usual source of silk, had broken down. Nylon was very strong and versatile. It could be woven into stockings and parachutes, or used for guitar strings or ropes.

❓ What Would YOU Do?

There are tons of plastic floating in oceans, where it sometimes forms into huge "garbage patches." Could you invent a machine that would be able to clear plastic from the ocean so it could be recycled, just like young Dutch inventor Boyan Slat is trying to do with his project, The Ocean Cleanup? Would you use a boat, a flying machine, or another kind of vehicle? Would you have a crew, or would a robot do the work?

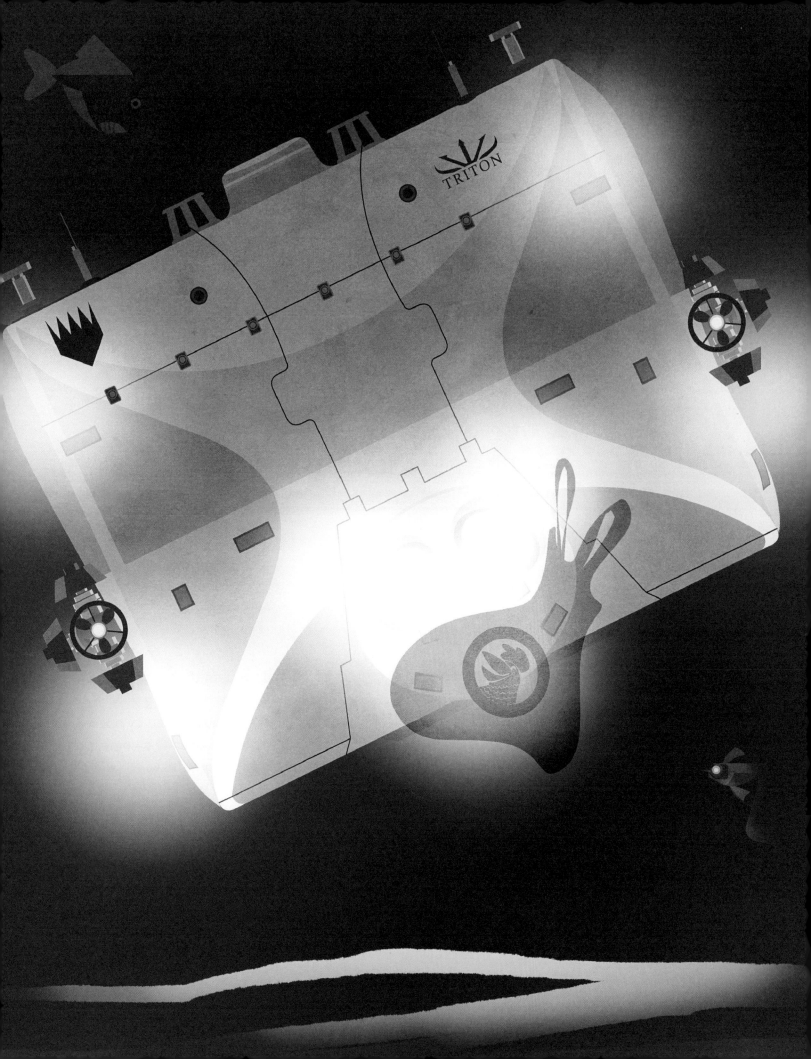

Vacuum Cleaner

If you're trying to relax and someone starts to vacuum around you, blame Hubert Cecil Booth. This British engineer built the first effective vacuum cleaner in 1901. At the time, there were cleaning machines that blew dirt away. He wondered if they could suck instead.

Puffing Billy

Booth put a damp handkerchief over his mouth and sucked hard at a cloth chair until the handkerchief was covered in dust. He turned this idea into a machine, which worked by creating a partial vacuum that sucked in air.

The vacuum—nicknamed "Puffing Billy"—was too big to fit indoors. It was pulled by horses and parked outside the customer's home. Long tubes were passed through the windows to clean the carpets inside. Within a year, Booth was cleaning King Edward VII's carpets.

That Really Sucks!

A more practical vacuum appeared in 1907. The U.S. janitor and inventor James Spangler rigged up what he called a suction cleaner. The blades of an electric fan sucked dust up a tube

with brushes on the end attached to a broom handle. The dust was trapped in a pillow.

Spangler didn't get the credit for his device. He sold the patent to William Hoover, who made some improvements and started selling the machines. His name stuck in Britain, where vacuums cleaners became known as "hoovers."

❓ What Would YOU Do?

Try vacuuming your home. No, seriously. Are there places your vacuum cannot reach? Is there anything that it will not pick up? Could it be easier to use? List the ways your vacuum could be improved. How easy would it be to make those improvements?

╋ Meet the Inventor · James Dyson Born 1947

In 1978 the British engineer James Dyson set out to invent a vacuum cleaner without a bag. He built 5,127 prototypes over five years before he got it right. His design sucks air into "cyclones" that spin out dust, which falls into a collection bin. The vacuum bag was history.

It took almost a decade for Dyson's invention to go into production—but within two years, it was the most successful vacuum cleaner on the market.

Dishwasher

Oven, refrigerator, blender, toaster: many handy kitchen tools and gadgets have been invented to save us time and make our lives easier. Are you lucky enough to have a dishwasher in your home? It's a real luxury. Instead of having to wash dishes by hand after a meal, you can relax and put your feet up as your food digests, while your plates become sparkling clean.

Doing the Dishes

The woman we have to thank for this invention is Josephine Cochrane. She didn't come up with idea of a dishwasher–but she created the first one that actually worked.

A patent for a machine to do the dishes was first awarded to the U.S. inventor Joel Houghton in 1850, for a machine that was cranked by hand. The only problem was that it didn't clean the dishes well enough.

Cochrane, meanwhile, was enjoying life in a mansion in Chicago with her family. She despaired that her beautiful china got chipped when the servants washed it. After she tried washing the dishes herself–she didn't enjoy it–she decided to come up with a better way.

Fixing the Problem

Cochrane had no scientific background, but she took a practical approach. Working with a mechanic, she measured her plates and cups and built wire compartments to hold them. The compartments were placed in a flat wheel inside a large copper boiler. A motor turned the wheel while jets of hot soapy water knocked food off the dishes. That set the basic design for all dishwashers since.

Cochrane received a patent for her machine in 1886. She sold machines to her wealthy friends, but most homes did not have as much hot water as the machine needed, so her main customers were restaurants and hotels. She continued to refine her designs, and produce new models.

The home dishwasher remained rare until the 1950s, when hot-water plumbing became more common and detergents improved–and more women decided that there were better ways to spend their time than with their hands in the sink.

❓ What Would YOU Do?

Look around your kitchen. Is there anything you can think of that still needs an invention to help? How about pouring out your cereal or scrambling an egg? What type of invention could perform a useful job in the kitchen?

5.

Making Us Better

Medical Inventions

Medical inventions have led to people living longer, healthier, happier lives. That's pretty amazing, right? But they're not all modern ideas—the ancient Egyptians came up with a simple invention for people who had lost toes or fingers in accidents. They carved a false body part from wood and attached it in place. That was the start of a history of prosthetics that led to the running blades you'll see in this chapter. Other medical advances that have changed our lives include ways to make surgery easier, microscopes that let us look at tiny cells, and methods to see inside the human body.

Microscope

You've probably seen images that make flies look like space monsters when viewed through a microscope. But before microscopes allowed us to look at things smaller than the naked human eye can see, no one knew that an extraordinary microscopic world even existed.

The Dutchman Hans Jansen and his son, Zacharias, were eyeglass makers who ground glass lenses to help people see better. In the 1590s, they put two lenses together in a tube. The device made things seem up to nine times bigger. It was the first microscope.

Seeing Too Much?

The church said that humans should see the world only with their own eyes, as God intended. But people were too curious to resist the new device. About 20 years later, the Italian scientist Galileo Galilei said: "With this tube, I have seen flies that look as big as lambs, and have learned that they are covered with hair."

Worlds Within Worlds

In 1665 English scientist Robert Hooke published a book of drawings of things as seen under a microscope. He drew the eyes of a fly and the tiny compartments in a piece of wood. He called the compartments "cells." We now know cells are the basic structures of all living things.

A few years later a cloth merchant from the Netherlands invented his own microscope for examining cloth. Antonie van Leeuwenhoek eventually made 550 lenses, the most powerful of which may have been able to magnify objects by 500 times. He saw tiny creatures in a drop of water (which were actually bacteria that can cause disease) and the cells in human blood. The letters he sent to scientists in London, England, describing his discoveries made him famous throughout Europe.

The microscope has become an essential tool in medicine (and other sciences). Among other things, it led to the discovery of germs and ways to prevent their spread. It also lets people study how the human body responds to diseases so that they can be treated more effectively.

Smaller and Smaller

Microscopes that use normal light can only magnify things to a certain limit. In the 1930s the German physicists Ernst Ruska and Max Knoll realized that a microscope didn't have to use light at all! They used beams of electrons to create images in a new type of microscope. Today, electron microscopes can magnify objects up to 1,000,000 times bigger than they are.

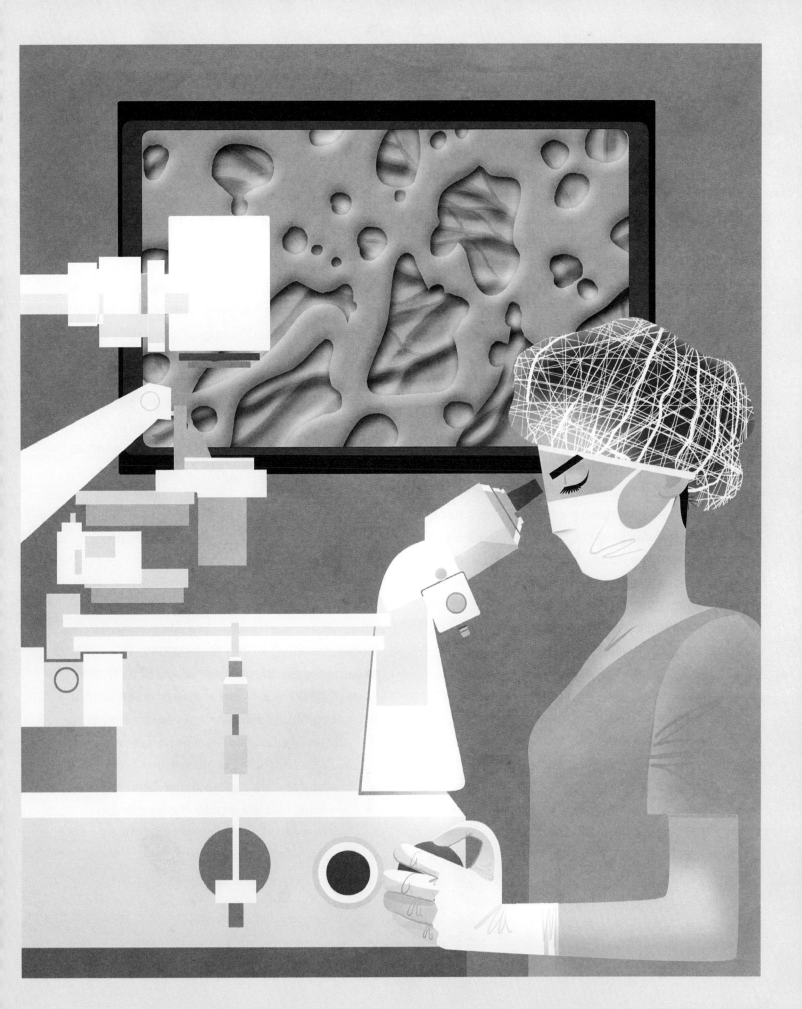

Pacemaker

Your heart beats about 80 times a minute. That's 42 million beats a year. By the time you're 12, your heart has beaten more than 500 million times; by the time you reach 20, it will be over 800 million. In most people, the beat is regular, although it speeds up and slows down depending on what they're doing. For some people, though, their heartbeat is erratic. It jumps around and sometimes . . . just . . . stops.

Having an erratic heartbeat is not good news. (Obviously, having it stop is even worse news.) But doctors can now reduce that risk. In 1926 the Australian doctor Mark Lidwill came up with an electrical device connected to a needle. The device was plugged into an electric light socket, and the needle was used to deliver an electric charge to one of the four chambers of the patient's heart. Even a small charge could kick the heart back into a regular pattern of beating. Lidwill used his machine to save a baby born without a heartbeat.

The Heart of the Matter

Lidwill's device, and a similar machine invented by the American Albert Hyman, were outside the body. They were not portable, so there was no chance of the patient living a normal life. Even when a wearable pacemaker was invented, the wearer's activity was greatly limited. It was in a plastic box hung around the neck.

But in 1958 the Swedish engineer Rune Elmqvist built a pacemaker at the direction of the surgeon Ake Senning. This device had a monitor for the heart rate and wires to apply an electrical charge from a small battery. But Elmqvist's big breakthrough was that the device could be implanted into the body. The first batteries only lasted two or three years, but today, lithium iodide batteries mean that a new pacemaker only has to be refitted every ten years or so.

+ Meet the Patient · Arne Larsson (1915–2001)

The first man to receive an internal pacemaker was Arne Larsson, whose heart beat so slowly that he often fainted. He had to be resuscitated up to 30 times a day. The first pacemaker Senning fitted was about the size of a hockey puck, and it failed within three hours. However, a replacement device lasted for two days. Larsson had another 25 operations to update his pacemakers–but they kept him alive until the age of 86. In fact, he lived longer than both Elmqvist and Senning!

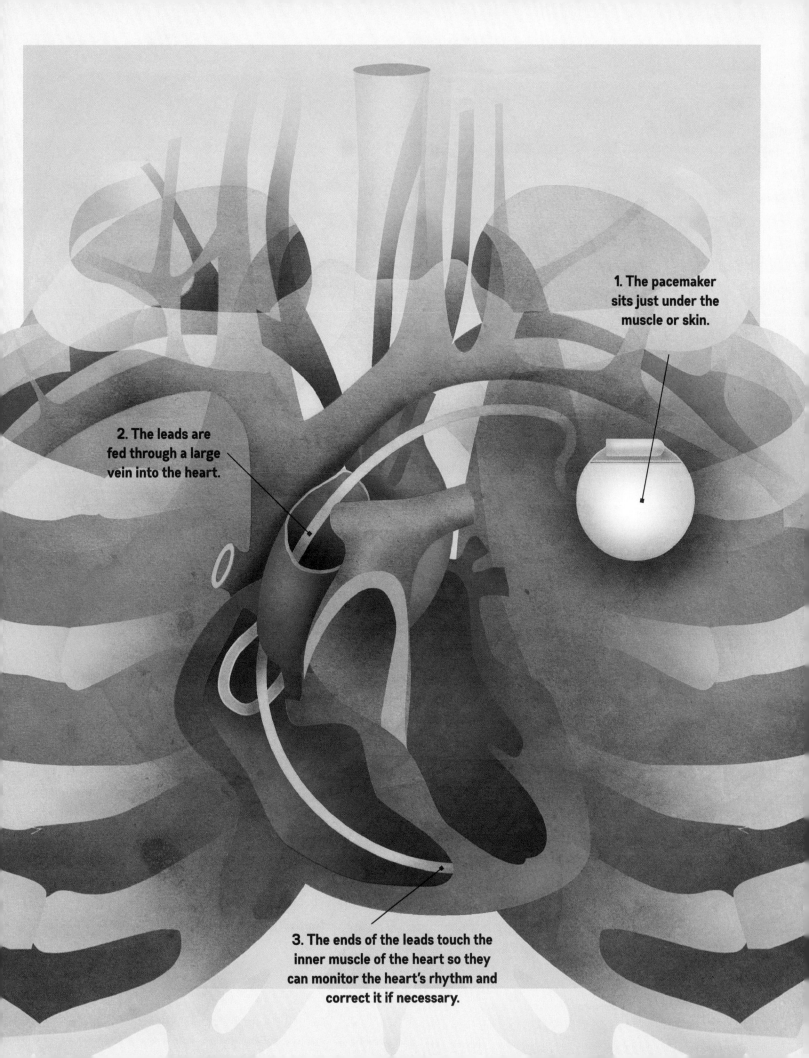

1. The pacemaker sits just under the muscle or skin.

2. The leads are fed through a large vein into the heart.

3. The ends of the leads touch the inner muscle of the heart so they can monitor the heart's rhythm and correct it if necessary.

Prosthetic Running Blades

From wooden legs to heavy plastic prosthetics (artificial body parts), for most of history, living without a limb made it very difficult and often painful to move around. However, modern inventions have now made it possible for a person without one or both legs to run, skip, and jump. In fact, top Paralympic athletes can often run faster than someone with two legs!

So how do these high-tech prosthetics work? They don't use any fancy robotics or electronics, just simple physics and the runner's own muscle power. Have you ever pushed down on a coiled spring and watched it bounce up when it's released? A running blade works in the same way. When a runner's blade hits the ground, it is squashed down, just like pressing down on a spring. Because the runner's leg can't move through the ground, her muscle power stops being kinetic (movement) energy and is instead stored as potential energy in the blade. This energy pushes the blade back up, propelling the runner forward.

Meet the Inventor · Van Phillips
Born 1954

American inventor Van Phillips lost his own leg in a waterskiing accident when he was 21. Unsatisfied with the prosthetic legs available, he decided to study prosthetics at Northwestern University Medical School in Chicago. Phillips then went on to become a biomedical design engineer, and in 1984 he started his own company, Flex-Foot, Inc., which created the very first running blades.

What Are the Blades Made From?

Running blades are made from carbon fiber, since this special—and expensive—material is incredibly lightweight but strong. It is made out of a kind of plastic mixed with fibers of carbon. To make the blades, as many as 90 thin sheets of carbon fiber are pressed together in a mold and fused at a very high temperature into a single piece. The blade is then cut to the correct shape and bolted to a socket designed to exactly fit the athlete's leg.

X-ray Machine

Have you ever wondered why X-rays are called X-rays? It's because in math "X" often stands for something that's unknown —and when he discovered X-rays in 1895, the German physicist Wilhelm Röntgen didn't know what they were.

Röntgen was experimenting with cathode rays, which are invisible beams of electrons inside an almost airless tube that create images on a screen coated with chemicals. He noticed that rays that hit the glass of the tube created a new form of radiation. He named them X-rays and tried to find out what they were. Röntgen's experiments showed that X-rays could pass through soft materials and leave an image on a photographic plate coated with the chemical barium.

Death Rays
Röntgen beamed the rays through paper and fabric . . . and then had an idea. What about the human body? His wife, Anna Bertha, put her hand on a photographic plate while Röntgen took the first radiograph of a human being. The X-rays passed through her flesh, but not through the bones of her hand, which showed

up clearly on the plate. Anna Bertha exclaimed, "I have seen my death!"

X-tremely Useful

Today, scientists know that X-rays are a type of electromagnetic radiation with a very short wavelength. When the rays hit atoms, they produce electrified particles called ions, which create the X-ray images. X-rays are extremely useful. They were used by English scientist Rosalind Franklin to take images of DNA (see page 94). But X-rays can damage the cells of the body. Today, anyone who works with X-rays uses protective clothing and screens.

Medical Use

In 1913, the U.S. physicist William Coolidge learned to use a form of tungsten in a glass tube designed to emit X-rays. For the first time, this allowed physicians to create powerful and stable X-rays that they could control accurately. That made X-rays a lot safer to use for both patients and doctors. It led to the rapid development of radiology —the use of X-rays in medicine—during World War I, when it saved the lives of many wounded soldiers.

MRI Scanner

Magnets are remarkable things. With a magnet, you can stick a note to a metal refrigerator door. You can make a compass. Oh, and you can see inside someone else's head—or even your own head!

Magnetic resonance imaging (MRI) allows doctors to look inside the human body without cutting it open, which is a very good thing—especially for the patients. Experiments in the 1950s and 1960s showed that bombarding the body with magnetic energy caused hydrogen atoms in the body's cells to start wobbling, or resonating.

As the excited atoms stopped wobbling, they generated faint radio waves. In theory, it would be possible to convert these waves into images.

Patently Useless

However, it wasn't until 1971 that a doctor in New York City named Raymond Damadian thought about building a magnetic resonance machine. He realized that the radio waves given off by diseased cells lasted longer than those from healthy cells, and suggested that MRI could help doctors locate tumors and cancers. A year later, he applied for a patent for an MRI

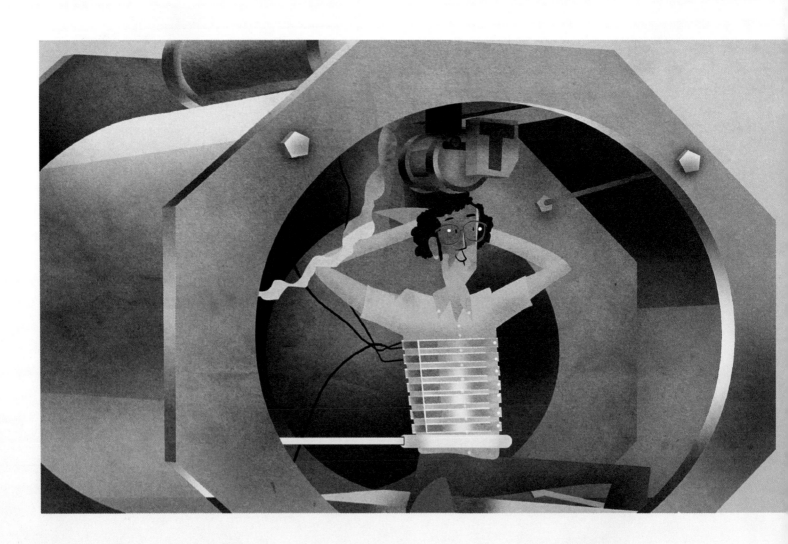

scanner. There was just one problem: no one knew how to build a machine that would be practical to use.

Look Inside Larry

Two other scientists helped. Paul Lauterbur used a varied or gradated magnetic field that made it easier to tell which cells were resonating. That produced better images, but the process took hours and the scans were still unclear. Peter Mansfield used complex math to figure out a new method that would take only seconds and produce sharper images. Using these breakthroughs, Damadian built the first scanning machine for the human body in 1977. The first human MRI scan showed the chest of his assistant, Larry Minkoff.

Inside the Body

Inventors have come up with numerous ways to see inside the human body. In ultrasound scans, high-frequency sound waves reflect off soft internal organs to create an image. Ultrasound is often used to examine fetuses developing in the womb. Computed tomography, meanwhile, puts together X-ray cross-sections to build a 3D image of the body. Positron emission tomography (PET) is a way to study activity in the brain by injecting the patient with a (weak!) radioactive substance.

Cataract Laser Surgery

Do you have a science kit? It could be the first step to becoming an inventor. Patricia Bath became interested in science when her mom gave her a chemistry set. As an adult, she invented new ways to perform eye surgery that improved the sight of many thousands of patients.

Of course, quite a lot happened between the chemistry set and the inventions—mainly a lot of hard work. Bath's father was the first African-American driver on the New York subway system, and at home in Harlem he and Patricia's mother encouraged their children to follow their ambitions.

After finishing high school in less than three years, Bath got a medical degree before going on to study ophthalmology (eye care, to you and me). She discovered that African-Americans suffered far more eye problems than other Americans, so she set up a project to provide better eye care to the local community.

At the University of California, Los Angeles (UCLA), Bath introduced new ways of training ophthalmologists. In the early 1980s, she spent five years looking for a better way to treat one of the most common eye conditions: cataracts.

Correcting Cataracts

A cataract is a cloud in the lens of the eye that blurs or fades the vision. Cataracts cause blindness around the world, particularly in poorer communities. They can be removed by surgery, and some surgeons used sound waves to break up the lens of the eye, making the cataract easier to remove.

Patricia's idea was to use lasers to break up the lens. That meant the surgeon could make a far smaller cut in the eye, which recovered more quickly. The breakthrough helped improve the sight of many thousands of people around the world. Her invention was called the Laserphaco probe.

Laser surgery

"Laser" stands for "Light Amplification by Stimulated Emission of Radiation." It's a device that focuses photons of light into a beam that contains so much energy it can be used to cut through metal, to drill through teeth—and to perform surgery. The first laser was invented by Theodore Maiman in 1960, and in 1973 surgeons began using lasers to help correct people's vision by adjusting the lenses of their eyes.

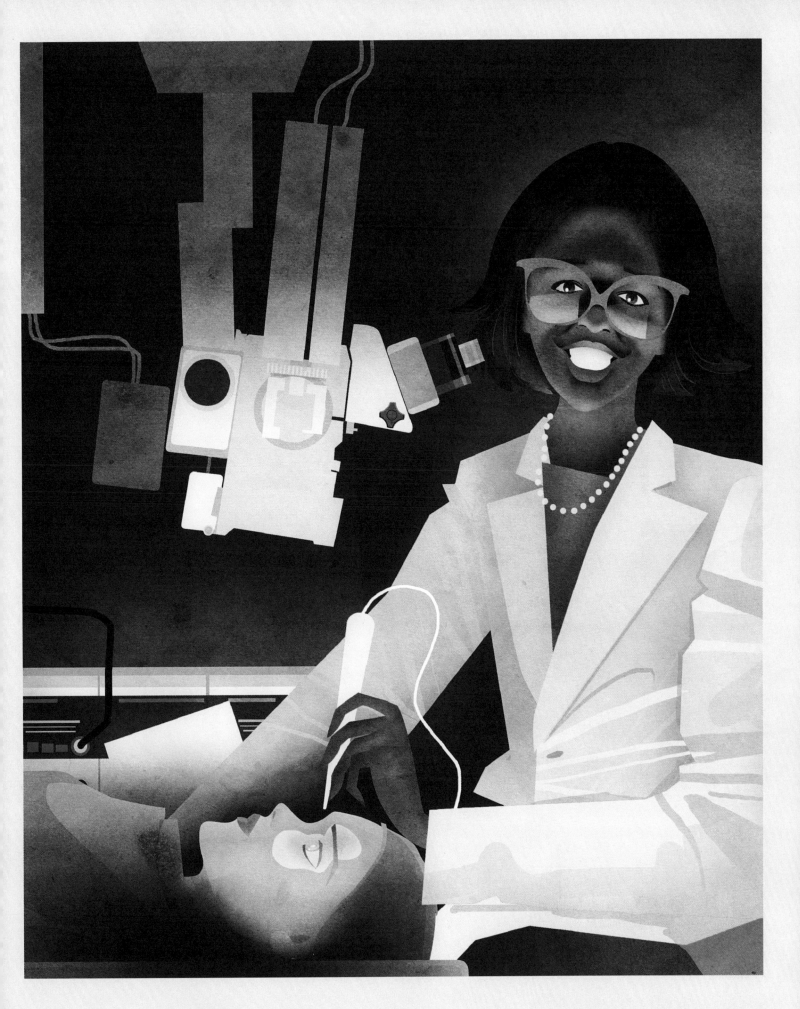

Making Us Safer

Accident & Crime-Busting Inventions

You should consider yourself lucky. Generally, the modern world is a pretty safe place to live. You are surrounded by inventions that take care of people, such as devices to keep you safe in a car or to warn you if your house is on fire. Technology can keep people safe, rescue them in case of disaster, and even discover people who have committed crimes.

Bulletproof Vest

Working for Jan Szczepanik was no fun. This Polish inventor used to fire revolvers at his servants to test whether the bulletproof vests that he made actually worked. Luckily for the servants, they did!

People started to invent ways to stop bullets almost as soon as guns were invented, around 1500. To start with, they wore metal suits of armor. Japanese armorers then figured out that layers of soft materials such as silk absorbed the shock of a bullet better.

Super Silk

Late in the 1800s, the U.S. physician George E. Goodfellow saw a gunfight. (He lived in Tombstone, Arizona, one of the most violent towns in the Wild West, where there were gunfights a lot of the time.) One man's life was saved when a silk handkerchief folded up in his pocket stopped a bullet. Goodfellow suggested it would be possible to make bulletproof vests with up to 30 layers of silk. The problem was that such a vest would have cost more than most people earned in a year.

Investing in Vests

During the world wars of the twentieth century, body armor improved rapidly. Iron was abandoned as being too heavy, and silk as being too expensive. Eventually, bulletproof vests came to be made of panels of lightweight plastic or ceramics, held in a vest of quilted nylon.

The big breakthrough came in 1965, when the U.S. chemist Stephanie Kwolek invented a new plastic called Kevlar. Material made from Kevlar was five times stronger than steel, yet it was very light. Vests made from Kevlar could not only stop bullets, but also knives. That made kevlar very popular with the military and the police!

+ Meet the Inventor · Stephanie Kwolek (1923–2014)

Kwolek was a chemist at the DuPont Corporation in the United States. She was trying to create new artificial materials when she accidentally produced a cloudy liquid. Kwolek tried spinning it out to make thin fibers. The result was Kevlar, which has now been used to make more than a million bulletproof vests. Kwolek said of her invention, "I don't think there's anything like saving someone's life to bring you satisfaction and happiness."

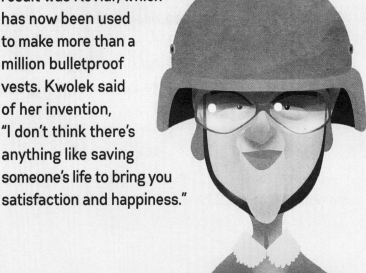

Fingerprinting

In 1892 Francisca Rojas's young son and daughter were killed at home in a village in Argentina. A few days later, a police officer found a fingerprint in a spot of dried blood. The officer had been trained in a new method of studying fingerprints—and he matched this one to Francisca Rojas. She was the first criminal to be found guilty thanks to fingerprint evidence.

Look closely at your fingers. The ends are covered with tiny friction ridges, which help you grip things. There are three basic patterns:

loops, circular whorls, and arches. Within these patterns, tiny variations make everyone's fingerprints unique. This means fingerprints are a reliable way to identify an individual. (That's why tech manufacturers use fingerprint scanners to let people unlock computers or smartphones.)

That's Criminal!

Fingerprints were used for identification in ancient China, and later in Persia. In the 1700s and 1800s, Europeans began trying to learn more about fingerprints. In 1877, an American

microscopist named Thomas Taylor suggested that it might be possible to identify criminals from their fingerprints.

Everyone's skin has a natural covering of grease (yuck!). When we touch anything, we leave traces. Most of the time these traces are invisible, though fingerprints are easy to see on clean glass. They can be made visible by dusting them with fine powder. It sticks to the grease, picking out the pattern of swirls.

Alphonse Bertillon, a French policeman, began to keep a card database of criminals' measurements, including fingerprints. Today, fingerprints are checked by computer against details of hundreds of thousands of people.

A police officer in Argentina named Juan

Vucetich read about Bertillon's work. He was intrigued and started to teach his officers to use fingerprints–unluckily for Francisca Rojas!

+ Meet the Inventor · Juan Vucetich (1858–1925)

Juan Vucetich's job was to identify criminals using a system of measurements like those of Bertillon. He thought he could see a better way to do it, using fingerprints, as it was thought that the chances of two fingerprints being the same were 1 in 64 million. Vucetich started taking fingerprints of criminals– and training the Argentine police in fingerprint identification.

DNA "Fingerprinting"

In 1988, a British man named Colin Pitchfork was convicted of murdering two teenage girls. The main evidence against him didn't come from witnesses but from a forensic scientist. Pitchfork was the first person found guilty by the new technique of "fingerprinting" a person's genetic makeup.

Deoxy What?

Genetic fingerprinting is based on something commonly known as DNA (or to give it its full name, deoxyribonucleic acid). It makes up the genes that are contained in every cell in a person's body. The genes instruct the cells on how to manufacture proteins—and the instructions they give are what make everyone similar to their own family and yet also unique.

English chemist Rosalind Franklin helped discover the structure of DNA in 1952, by taking a picture of it that showed its pattern. But she wasn't credited with her discovery at the time—the credit went to other scientists who used her picture to help their research.

All in the Genes

All people share 99.9 percent of their DNA, but in 1984 a British biochemist named Alec Jeffreys realized that the variation in the remaining DNA could be used to identify individuals.

Family Resemblance

Jeffreys was studying patterns in DNA called minisatellites, which are parts of the DNA sequence that are very variable (unlike the boring 99.9 percent). Jeffreys was trying to find out if these areas could tell him anything about disease. He put DNA from individuals from the same family on X-ray film and saw that the patterns were similar enough to show that they were all related—but different enough to show that they were all unique. Although the film looked like a mess, Jeffreys later said that it took him less than 30 minutes to realize that DNA could be used to identify individuals.

Jeffreys's evidence helped convict Pitchfork. But it also proved that another man, who had confessed to the murders, could not be guilty. The technology proved someone guilty and someone innocent in the same case! No wonder police and lawyers everywhere started using DNA evidence.

+ Meet the Scientist · Margarita Salas Falgueras (1938-2019)

Imagine there's a tiny amount of blood or hair left at a crime scene. The DNA inside it might provide the clue to who was there—but there isn't enough DNA in it to test. That's where the Italian scientist Margarita Salas Falgueras's work comes in handy. She figured out a reliable and simple way to turn tiny amounts of DNA into large enough amounts to test.

Driving Safety

There are about one billion cars in the world. Unfortunately, sometimes they are driven by people who aren't paying attention. Accidents happen, but two inventions in the middle of the twentieth century made cars far safer to drive: the seat belt and the airbag.

The first seat belt was not designed for a car but for one of the first flying machines. In the mid-1800s George Cayley invented a belt to hold him in his glider, a little like a seat belt on a modern airliner.

Three Is the Magic Number

By the 1950s, belts like Cayley's were being used in cars. However, cars were much faster than gliders. Nils Bohlin, the safety engineer for the Swedish car company Volvo worried that the single-strap seat belt would cause injury in a high-speed crash. In 1959 he designed a new belt that the wearer could put on with one hand. It strapped across the wearer's chest as well as the waist. It was fixed at three points—behind the shoulder and at waist level on either side of the seat.

The three-point seat belt reduced the chances of dying in a car crash by at least 50 percent. For the sake of safety, Volvo let other companies use it for free. By 2009, it was estimated that the invention had saved at least a million lives.

Blow Up!

Around the same time, an American engineer named John W. Hetrick was inspired to invent the airbag when he almost crashed his car. As he slammed on the brakes, he and his wife instinctively threw out their arms to try to stop their daughter from flying forward. He decided that an airbag could do the same job.

In the U.S. Navy, Hetrick had seen compressed air from a torpedo inflate a canvas bag. That became the starting point for his invention. He wanted to put bags in cars that filled with gas if the vehicle stopped suddenly. The bags would cushion people thrown forward in a crash. He patented his invention in 1953, but it was decades before airbags were routinely included in cars.

Fire Engine

No one knows who invented the first fire engine, but it may have been in ancient Rome. We do know, however, that it didn't have a siren or a ladder, and it was unlikely to have been red. More likely, it was a cart or wheelbarrow that carried buckets of water or sand. That might not sound like much, but if your house was on fire, you'd still be pleased to see it!

The Romans used hand pumps to squirt water through tubes from a tank on a cart. Men used buckets to keep the tank filled with water. This vehicle, called a hand tub, set the model for fire engines for centuries. Fire was a terrifying threat in cities full of wooden buildings that burned easily. In 1666, a fire destroyed more than 13,000 homes in London, England—despite the city's mayor suggesting when it started that it was so small, someone could pee on it to put it out!

Bucket List

The immediate forerunners of modern fire engines were built in the 1600s, and more appeared in cities in England and North

America in the 1700s. They still relied on buckets to keep the tank full, and they had to be dragged by hand to the site of the blaze (horses were too sensible to go near a burning building).

Steaming Hot

The 1800s brought a series of improvements. First, fire engines started using a steam engine to suck water from ponds or special reservoirs. Then, steam-driven pumps were used to shoot water farther, so fire engines did not need to get so close to a fire–that meant horses were happier to pull them! Horses were replaced by gasoline engines around 1900.

What's a Fire Engine?

Fire engines that carry water and hoses are called pumpers. Other fire vehicles have also appeared. Once the first skyscrapers were built in the late 1800s, trucks were built to carry extending ladders. Some trucks also have turntables, so the ladders can face any direction. Other fire engines have long arms with platforms on the end to rescue people from heights.

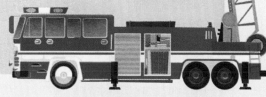

Smoke Detector

Do you ever get annoyed when you burn your toast and the ear-piercing noise of the smoke alarm makes you jump? Well don't. Be thankful instead—the risk of dying in a house fire is cut in half if you have a working smoke detector. Smoke detectors sound an alarm when they detect smoke, which is made from particles of carbon and gases released when something burns. And there's no smoke without fire!

Better with Butter?

George A. Darby, an electrical engineer in Birmingham, England, in the early 1900s, came up with an unlikely way to warn people of a fire: butter. Darby built an electrical circuit with two metal plates separated by a block of butter. As the heat rose, the butter melted and the two plates came into contact, closing the circuit and sounding the alarm (while making everyone think of fresh popcorn). Darby's heat detector was not very practical. By the time the butter melted, the fire was probably well established.

What a Gas!

The first sign of a fire is often smoke, not heat. (Smoke is also the biggest danger in a fire— breathing it in causes the majority of deaths in fires.) In 1939 a Swiss physicist named Ernst Meili invented a device to detect the presence of poisonous gases in mines. Canaries everywhere probably gave a chirp of relief because, in the past, miners had used these birds to test the air underground. If the bird died, it was time to get out. Meili's device was an ionization chamber. It produces a stream of electrically charged atoms—ions—between two poles called electrodes. The presence of gas, such as smoke, breaks the stream and an alarm sounds.

Smoke Gets in Your (Photoelectric) Eyes

Meili's device was soon being used to detect smoke. Too large for the home, it was used in factories in the 1950s, but a smaller, battery-powered version was patented in 1969. A few years later, Donald Steele and Robert Enemark in the United States came up with an even more sensitive photoelectric smoke detector. This detector measures whether beams of light that it projects are being disturbed by particles of smoke in the air.

Saved by the Bell

Today, the most effective smoke detectors combine ionization technology with photoelectric smoke detection. The technology behind them is complicated, but ionization-type alarms generally respond to fires that have big flames, and photoelectric alarms react to smoldering fires, with less fierce flames.

Rescue Robot

Imagine you're trapped in a collapsed building after an earthquake. After a while, you hear a sound and turn on a flashlight. It must be rescuers digging you out. Then, creeping through small holes in the rubble, come what look like large cockroaches! Do you a) celebrate, b) scream, or c) pass out?

It might sound like a joke (or even a nightmare), but this is the vision of inventors at the University of California at Berkeley. Those "cockroaches" are tiny robots that adopt the characteristics of real cockroaches—even

having a shell-like outer covering—to explore disaster sites looking for survivors. The robots are called CRAMs (short for "compressible robot with articulated mechanisms").

Animal Inspiration
CRAM is one of the latest in a line of robots designed for situations too dangerous for humans. Modern rescue robots can operate in almost any environment. Velox, which can rescue people from dangerously cold water such as frozen lakes, resembles a type of sea creature known as a mollusk. Snakebot has a

long, thin body made up of 12 joints, allowing it to crawl through small spaces or even up trees.

Robot Wars

Aerial drones can deliver supplies to disaster regions, search for missing persons, or even start controlled avalanches in the mountains by deliberately detonating explosives. Other robots are used for firefighting—like Colossus and the Thermite RS1 and RS2, which can get close to fires and blast out huge amounts of water or foam. Zebro, meanwhile, is a small land-based robot that operates in "swarms," or groups, to explore disaster scenes to search for survivors. At sea, remote-controlled robotic lifeboats have been used to rescue migrants.

❓ What Would YOU Do?

For people used to science-fiction movies, it might be disappointing that most rescue robots don't look like humans—or even have a humanoid shape. There are good reasons, however. The robots often have to be able to squeeze into small spaces or travel across rough ground. If you wanted to design your own rescue robot, you'd have to think about the features it would need to work in a particular environment. What shape would be best suited to the task? Which attachments would be useful?

Over to You

This section was originally going to be called "What Next?" But no one really knows what the next generation of inventions might be. When your parents were young, for example, they probably couldn't have imagined inventions that we rely on today, such as smartphones and drones.

The inventions that are just around the corner might not be predictable–but we do know that they will be developed by people like you. Young people who are curious about the world and observe things closely. People who see problems and want to solve them. People who notice where tiny changes might help individuals or industries– or the whole planet! So that's why we've retitled this section "Over to You"!

Facing Challenges

There's a proverb that says that necessity is the mother of invention. In other words, when you need to do something enough, you think of a way to do it. Well, humans have a lot of challenges to solve. One of the most urgent is to come up with new forms of renewable energy. Others are finding new nonpolluting materials, energy-efficient transportation, and ways to measure climate change. Such problems can feel overwhelming– but the history of human ingenuity suggests that we can ultimately solve them.

Starting Small

Not all the problems inventors tackle are huge. Take the American inventor Lily Born, who was only eight years old when she invented a no-spill cup for her grandfather, who has Parkinson's disease. It was simple but effective–she added legs to a normal cup. She didn't save the world, but she made a small difference.

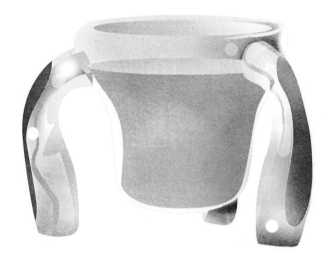

Get Inventing!

So that's your cue. You've seen all the "What Would You Do?" boxes in this book. Well, think about it. Would you start mixing up chemicals to try to invent a completely new substance– and what would you use it for? Would you take apart all the electrical devices in your parents' house and try to put them together to make something new? (You shouldn't!) Or would you go for a walk and try to spot things that could be improved? Could you make a road sign easier to see, or a pair of boots that are easier to put on?

The inventions in this book are just a drop in the ocean. Lots of things have already been invented, and lots of things have yet to be invented. So what are you waiting for?

Time Line

1600s

c. 1608 Hans Lippershey claims to have come up with a telescope

1820s

1826 Joseph Nicéphore Niépce takes the world's first permanent photograph

1840s

1843 Ada Lovelace designs the first computer program

1890s

1892 A murderer is convicted using fingerprint evidence for the first time

1894 Guglielmo Marconi sends the first wireless signals

1895 Wilhelm Röntgen discovers X-rays

1790s

1794 Robert Street invents the internal combustion engine

1829 Robert Stephenson builds the *Rocket* steam locomotive

1870s

1876 Alexander Graham Bell files a patent for the telephone

1876 Nikolaus Otto invents the four-stroke internal combustion engine

1850s

1856 Alexander Parkes invents the first successful plastic

1450s

1450 Johannes Gutenberg invents a printing press

1590 Hans and Zacharias Jansen build a working microscope

1596 John Harington invents the flushing lavatory

1590s

1712 Thomas Newcomen invents an early form of steam engine

1710s

1800 Alessandro Volta invents the first battery

1800s

1830 Charles Babbage invents a mechanical calculator

1838 Samuel Morse invents Morse code

1839 Edmond Becquerel describes the photovoltaic effect (the foundation of solar power)

1830s

1862 Étienne Lenoir builds a three-wheeled car

1860s

1880 The world's first coal-burning power plant starts producing electricity

1880s Mary Walton invents ways to decrease sound and smoke pollution from trains

1885 Karl Benz builds the three-wheeled Motorwagen car

1886 Josephine Cochrane invents a mechanical dishwasher

1889 George Eastman invents transparent film, greatly popularizing photography

1880s

1900 The first voice signals are transmitted by radio

1901 Hubert Cecil Booth invents the first vacuum cleaner

1903 The Wright brothers make the world's first powered flight in their airplane

1903 Marie and Pierre Curie receive a Nobel Prize for their discovery of radiation

1900s

1910s

1913 The first home refrigerator is invented in the United States by Fred W. Wolf

1913 William Coolidge develops a safe way to produce X-rays

1914 Florence Parpart invents her home refrigerator

1930s

1934 Wallace Carothers invents nylon

1938 Lise Meitner and Otto Hahn discover nuclear fission

1939 Igor Sikorsky invents the first successful helicopter

1950s

1952 Rosalind Franklin takes an image of the structure of DNA

1953 John W. Hetrick patents the airbag for cars

1954 The first color TV is introduced

1956 The world's first commercial nuclear power plant goes into operation

1957 Mary Sherman Morgan invents the rocket fuel Hydyne

1958 Rune Elmqvist and Ake Senning build the first modern pacemaker

1959 Nils Bohlin invents the three-point seat belt for cars

1970s

1977 Raymond Damadian takes the first MRI scan of the human body

1990s

1990 Tim Berners-Lee invents the World Wide Web

1993 The GPS system becomes operational

2000s

2007 Apple launches the first touch-screen smartphone

2008 The U.S. company Tesla introduces an electric car

1924 John Logie Baird uses a mechanical system to transmit TV images

1926 Robert Goddard launches the world's first rocket

1920s

1940s

1941 Konrad Zuse builds a programmable computer

1942 Enrico Fermi creates the first sustainable nuclear chain reaction

1942 Hedy Lamarr receives a patent for her frequency hopping technology which led to Wi-Fi

1960s

1960s Grace Hopper promotes the computer language COBOL

1965 Stephanie Kwolek invents Kevlar

1969 A space rocket launches into space the first humans to land on the Moon

1969 Marie Van Brittan Brown receives a patent for her home security system

1980s

1981 The first digital camera is introduced

1981 NASA's reusable space shuttle flies for the first time

1983 James Dyson invents the bagless vacuum cleaner

1984 The first maglev train becomes operational

1985 Olga González-Sanabria (and others) are granted a patent for long-life nickel hydrogen batteries

1988 DNA fingerprinting is used to convict a criminal for the first time in Britain

1988 Patricia Bath invents the Laserphaco probe to treat cataracts

1988 Margarita Salas Falgueras patents her DNA sampling technique

2010s

2011 Azza Abdel Hamid Faiad invents a new way to make biofuel from plastic

2016 Maanasa Mendu invents energy-gathering HARVEST device

2017 Google tests first driverless cars on public roads

Glossary

aeronautical–related to building aircraft

ammonia–a colorless, strong-smelling gas that dissolves in water and is often used as a cleaning fluid

artificial intelligence–the development of computer systems that can perform tasks that usually require human intelligence, such as making decisions or interpreting visual signals

bacteria–a large group of single-celled organisms that can cause disease

ball cock–a valve that opens and closes pipes in a water tank

biofuel–fuel made from organic (natural) matter

bitumen–a sticky black substance that occurs naturally or is produced during the manufacture of petroleum

cancers–diseases caused by the uncontrollable division of cells in parts of the body

carbon dioxide–a colorless, odorless gas produced by burning substances and by human exhalation (breathing out). It can contribute to global warming

cellulose–a substance that forms the walls of plant cells and vegetable fibers such as cotton

chain reaction–a chemical reaction in which the chemicals produced mean that the reaction continues to take place

closed-circuit camera–a camera that records images or video for security purposes

Cold War–a period of political hostility between the United States and the Soviet Union from 1945 to 1990

compass–a device that uses a magnetized needle for navigation

compressed air–air that is kept under high pressure

cyclone–a system of strong winds rotating around a central hub

digital–describes data that is stored in the form of the digits 0 and 1

discovery–the process of learning or understanding something that has not previously been understood

electrodes–poles through which electricity enters or leaves a substance such as liquid

electromagnets–metal cores that are made magnetic by electricity passing through wire coils wrapped around them

electrons–subatomic particles present in all atoms that carry a negative charge and that are the main means of transmitting an electrical current

energy–the ability to do work, or power to do work derived from physical or chemical sources

exhaust–waste gases left over by a chemical reaction

forensic–using scientific methods to try to solve crimes

fossil fuels–fuels such as coal and gas that were created millennia ago by the decay of vegetable matter such as plants

gasoline–a form of petroleum used as a fuel for internal combustion engines

generators–machines that convert mechanical energy, such as rotation, into electrical energy

genes–biological units that pass on characteristics from parents to their children

hydrofoil–a boat equipped with horizontal "wings" beneath it that lift the hull out of the water when it travels at high speed

Industrial Revolution–a period of rapid industrialization in Europe and North America in the late 1700s and early 1800s

integrated circuit–an electronic circuit formed on a small piece of semiconducting material, such as silicon

invention–a unique device or process that has been created by an individual or individuals

laser–a device that produces a powerful beam of light

locomotive–a powered rail vehicle used to pull train cars

mechanical–operated by a moving machine or machinery, rather than electronic or digital

molecule–a group of atoms that is joined together tightly

moons–celestial bodies that orbit planets

organs–structures in the body with specific purposes, such as the heart, lungs, and brain

patent–a license to be the only person who can create or sell a new invention for a set period of time

phonograph–an early form of record player

photons–particles that represent quanta, or "packets," of light or electromagnetic radiation

physics–the branch of science that studies the nature and properties of matter and energy

piston–a cylinder or disk that moves up and down inside a close-fitting tube

plastic–a synthetic material made from organic chemicals that can be molded into shape while soft and then sets into a hard or semi-elastic form

radiation–a form of high-energy electromagnetic waves that can harm living organisms

reservoirs–large natural or artificial lakes used as a water supply

robots–machines that can function automatically and that sometimes resemble human beings and human movements

sanitary–relating to conditions that promote hygiene and good health

satellites–artificial bodies placed in orbit around Earth

silicon–a nonmetal element used to make electrical circuits

superconductors–substances that can transport an electrical current very easily with no resistance

textile–a piece of cloth created by weaving yarn together

tumors–swellings in the body caused by an abnormal growth of tissue

turbines–machines that produce continuous power by revolving, usually driven by the wind, fast-flowing streams, steam, gas, or fluid.

vacuum–a space that contains nothing at all

valve–a device that controls the flow of an electrical current through a wire

Find Out More

Science & Invention
+ The Science Museum in London, England, with many online objects and stories:
www.sciencemuseum.org.uk

+ A time line of the history of science and invention:
https://www.explainthatstuff.com/timeline.html

+ An index page with links to biographies of some of the greatest of all inventors:
https://www.history.com/topics/inventions

Energy Inventions
+ A history of nuclear power from the World Nuclear Association:
https://www.world-nuclear.org/information-library/current-and-future-generation/outline-history-of-nuclear-energy.aspx

+ A page from the Royal Institution in London about the voltaic pile it was given by the inventor Alessandro Volta:
https://www.rigb.org/our-history/iconic-objects/iconic-objects-list/voltaic-pile

Transportation Inventions
+ The Wright brothers' breakthroughs in flight, and information about rockets and missiles from the Smithsonian National Air and Space Museum:
https://airandspace.si.edu/exhibitions/wright-brothers/online/ and
https://airandspace.si.edu/learn/highlighted-topics/rockets-and-missiles

Information and Communication Inventions
+ A biography of Guglielmo Marconi from the Nobel Prize organization, who gave him the prize in 1909:
https://www.nobelprize.org/prizes/physics/1909/marconi/biographical/

+ Alexander Graham Bell and the telephone:
https://www.sciencemuseum.org.uk/objects-and-stories/ahoy-alexander-graham-bell-and-first-telephone-call

+ About Tim Berners-Lee, World Wide Web inventor:
https://www.w3.org/People/Berners-Lee/

+ An article from the U.S. Library of Congress about Galileo and the early telescope:
https://www.loc.gov/collections/finding-our-place-in-the-cosmos-with-carl-sagan/articles-and-essays/modeling-the-cosmos/galileo-and-the-telescope

Household Inventions
+ A history of the flushing toilet:
https://www.baus.org.uk/museum/164/the_flush_toilet

Medical Inventions
+ How the invention of the microscope has helped us:
https://www.smithsonianmag.com/science-nature/what-we-owe-to-the-invention-microscope-180962725/

+ A rare X-ray by Wilhelm Röntgen, the inventor of X-rays, with information from the British Library:
https://www.bl.uk/learning/cult/bodies/xray/roentgen.html

Accident & Crime-Busting Inventions
+ The history of fingerprinting in forensic science:
https://science.howstuffworks.com/fingerprinting3.htm

+ An article to celebrate the millionth life saved by the three-point seat belt:
https://www.media.volvocars.com/uk/en-gb/media/pressreleases/20505

What's Next?
+ Fantastic inventions by young inventors:
https://www.bbc.com/future/article/20180316-four-teenage-inventors-changing-the-world and
https://greatbusinessschools.org/10-great-inventions-dreamt-up-by-children/

Index